Frances Perkins

Champion of the New Deal

OXFORD
PORTRAITS

Frances Perkins

Champion of the New Deal

Naomi Pasachoff

2/00 JB
perkins

Oxford University Press
New York • Oxford

*In loving memory of my father, Isaac Schwartz
(1912–1999), who shared with Frances Perkins a deep
commitment to social justice.*

Oxford University Press

Oxford   New York
Athens   Auckland   Bangkok   Bogotá   Buenos Aires   Calcutta
Cape Town   Chennai   Dar es Salaam   Delhi   Florence   Hong Kong   Istanbul
Karachi   Kuala Lumpur   Madrid   Melbourne   Mexico City   Mumbai
Nairobi   Paris   São Paulo   Singapore   Taipei   Tokyo   Toronto   Warsaw
and associated companies in
Berlin   Ibadan

Copyright © 1999 by Naomi Pasachoff
Published by Oxford University Press, Inc.
198 Madison Avenue, New York, New York 10016

Design and layout: Greg Wozney
Picture research: Amla Sanghvi

Library of Congress Cataloging-in-Publication Data

Pasachoff, Naomi E.
Frances Perkins : champion of the New Deal / Naomi Pasachoff.
p. cm.
Includes bibliographical references and index.
ISBN 0-19-512222-4 (acid-free paper)
1. Perkins, Frances, 1880-1965. 2. United States, Dept. of Labor Boigraphy.
3. Women cabinet officers—United States Biography. 4. Women social
reformers—United States Biography. 5. Labor movement—United States—
History. 6. Labor policy—United States—History. 7. Labor laws and
legislation—United States—History. 8. New Deal, 1933-1939. I. Title.
HD8073.P38P37   1999
973.917'092—dc21
[B]   99-27292

9 8 7 6 5 4 3 2 1

Printed in the United States of America
on acid-free paper

On the cover: Francis Perkins works at her desk at the Department of Labor in
Washington, D.C.
Frontispiece: Perkins witnesses President Franklin Roosevelt sign the Social
Security Act.

CONTENTS

PREFACE

In *The Roosevelt I Knew*, Frances Perkins's biography of Franklin D. Roosevelt, she wrote, "If this book can help to establish the real... leader by getting closer to the man himself, I shall feel that I have done him some service." Although I was not lucky enough to know Frances Perkins at all, and in writing her biography certainly could not draw on a 35-year social and professional connection like the one she had with Roosevelt, I hope, nonetheless, that this book will provide readers a service by bringing them closer to the remarkable woman who is its subject.

Throughout *The Roosevelt I Knew*, there is much material that sheds light on Perkins's own life and achievement. The chapter titles for the present book all come from her Roosevelt biography. An even richer source for Perkins's biographer, however, is *The Reminiscences of Frances Perkins*, a series of long interviews she gave under the auspices of Columbia University's Oral History Research Office over a four-year period in the 1950s. Except where otherwise indicated, all quotations from Perkins in this book come from the transcripts of the oral history.

Elected in her final year at Mount Holyoke to the position of permanent president of the class of 1902, "Perk" led the Ivy Day ceremony before commencement.

THE PURSUIT OF SOCIAL JUSTICE WOULD BE MY VOCATION

The man who had been elected President of the United States three months earlier was hardly a stranger to Frances Perkins. She had known him socially for over 20 years. Active herself in Democratic politics, she had, since 1912, watched him participate in the national conventions every four years. She had followed from a distance—with sympathy and interest—his battle with polio, which he had contracted in August 1921 and which left him disabled. Most recently he had been her boss for four years. Together they had worked to alleviate the desperate economic situation that had befallen their state of New York, as it had the rest of the country.

While she prepared for the appointment she had for this late February evening, many things went through her mind. She knew why the meeting had been arranged. For nearly two months now a rumor had been circulating that the former governor of New York wanted to take to Washington as his secretary of labor the woman who, as Industrial Commissioner, had headed his state's Department of Labor for the two terms he had served.

The thought of moving to Washington distressed her

deeply, for a variety of personal and professional reasons. But her grandmother had taught her many years earlier that when opportunity opens a door, only a fool resists walking through it. Nonetheless, before she accepted the offer she had to know if the President-elect would support her in advocating the programs she would wish to pursue as secretary of labor.

Therefore, shortly after being ushered into his study, as soon as he had confirmed the purpose of the meeting, she pulled out the little slip of paper she had prepared for the occasion. On it she had jotted down the list of goals about which she felt passionate. Among other items on the list were laws for minimum wages and maximum hours, for unemployment insurance and old-age insurance. As she had learned to do over the years she had worked for him, she spelled out very clearly the items she would fight for if she became a member of his Cabinet, so that there would be no question of misunderstanding. Then she asked, "Are you sure that you want this done, because you won't want me for Secretary of Labor if you don't.... I'd be an embarrassment to you.... You wouldn't want me if you didn't want that done."

Only when he firmly answered, "I'll back you," could she think about putting aside her hesitation and accepting the offer.

And so, less than two weeks later, on March 4, 1933, Frances Perkins became the first woman to serve in the United States Cabinet when she was sworn in along with Franklin D. Roosevelt's other appointees. The legacy of her years in office continues to affect the life of every U.S. citizen.

Fannie Coralie Perkins, as she was named at birth, was born in Boston on April 10, 1880, to Fred W. Perkins and Susan Bean Perkins, who were both descended from early British settlers of New England. Her birth certificate lists her father's occupation as "periodical dealer." When Fanny (as the family more regularly spelled her name) was two, the Perkinses moved to Worcester, a city in central Massachusetts, where her father did quite well in the stationery business. Although her father had never gone to college, he was a very well-read man. Perkins described her father as "quite a scholar in the field of law" and recalled his reading ancient Greek "for pleasure" and teaching it to her when she was only eight.

While the love of learning that eventually awakened in Perkins may be traced back to her father, she attributed to her mother not only her lifelong interest in art but also the style of hat that later became her professional trademark. When Fanny was 12, her mother took her to Lamston and Hubbard, one of Boston's finest millinery shops. Her mother picked out a tricorn—a hat with the brim turned up on three sides, in the style favored by the early American colonists. Placing it on her daughter's head, she said, "There, my dear, that is your hat. You should always wear a hat something like this. You have a very broad face.... Never let yourself get a hat that is narrower than your cheekbones, because it makes you look ridiculous."

Pensive and dreamy, four-year-old Fanny poses for a portrait in a rustic setting.

Neither of Fanny's parents seems to have been concerned with bolstering her self-confidence about her looks. She once told a friend what her father had said when she tried on a new party dress: that the dress was ladylike, though it did not make her look pretty. According to Perkins, even if she had ever looked pretty, her parents would never have told her so. They would have considered any such preoccupation with physical beauty to be sinful. Yet despite both parents' harsh comments on Fanny's looks, she grew up with enormous affection and respect for both of them.

Fanny had only one sibling, a sister, Ethel, who was four years younger. What seems to have most impressed her older sister was Ethel's "extraordinarily bad temper as a child." The other members of the Perkins family seemed to value peaceful relations more than absolute honesty, so that "if somebody sold you out and did you dirty, you should keep a perfectly calm face and be very pleasant." Ethel, on the other hand, refused to keep her true feelings under wraps merely to present "a good picture to the outside world." Years later Perkins would sometimes witness important industrialists display fits of temper in their handling of labor disputes. The thought of how Ethel had eventually learned to tame her temper convinced Perkins that these grown men could also learn to handle themselves in a more socially acceptable manner.

Also important in shaping Perkins's character was her relationship with her father's mother, Cynthia Otis Perkins, a descendant of the colonial statesman James Otis, who is said to have coined the phrase "Taxation without representation is tyranny." Together with her family Fanny visited Grandmother Perkins every summer at the family home in Newcastle, Maine, on the Damariscotta River. Although neither was aware of any special nature to the relationship, Perkins recounted as an adult that hardly a day went by when she was not guided by the memory of some piece of wisdom her grandmother had casually imprinted on her impressionable granddaughter decades earlier.

Fanny did not shine as a pupil at school, but in an age when few women were educated beyond high school her parents enrolled her in the one Worcester public high school that prepared its students for admission to college. After graduating from Worcester Classical High School in June 1898, Fanny left home for South Hadley, a town in western Massachusetts, to enroll at Mount Holyoke College that fall. The school had been founded 61 years earlier, originally as Mount Holyoke Female Seminary, by Mary Lyons, a pioneer in the field of higher education for women. The founder's goal was to train women to do meaningful and socially valuable work in the world. According to Lyon, "Education was to fit one to do good."

Like many young people leaving home for the relative freedom of college, Fanny hoped to enjoy many extracurricular and social activities at Mount Holyoke. "Perk," as her classmates came to know her, succeeded in involving herself in college dramatic productions. She often invited a high school friend, William Piper, now a student at nearby Amherst College, to Mount Holyoke functions. Although neither an athlete nor a sorority member, she became popular enough before graduating in 1902 to be elected permanent class president to represent her classmates over their postgraduate years. Many of the friendships she developed in college endured for a lifetime.

But Perk's professors did not let her growing social skills undermine the educational goals they had set for her. At Mount Holyoke she had to work harder than she had been accustomed to in high school. At Worcester Classical she had been able to get by in her Latin course, for example, by giving approximate translations of paragraphs. But Professor Esther Van Dieman at Mount Holyoke demanded precision of her freshman Latin students, and Perk "for the first time...became conscious of character." Drawn to history, literature, art, and language, she probably would not have taken chemistry at all if it had not been a required course. Professor Nellie Esther Goldthwaite's course proved very difficult for her, but, perhaps to prove to herself and others that she could succeed at it, she not only passed the course but also chose Dr. Goldthwaite as her advisor and chemistry as her major, with supporting work in physics and biology.

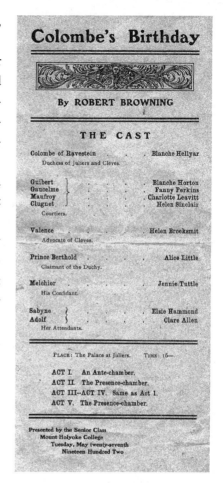

Colombe's Birthday

By ROBERT BROWNING

THE CAST

Colombe of Ravestein	Blanche Hellyar
Duchess of Juliers and Cleves.	
Guibert	Blanche Horton
Gaucelme	Fanny Perkins
Maufroy	Charlotte Leavitt
Clugnet	Helen Sinclair
Courtiers.	
Valence	Helen Broeksmit
Advocate of Cleves.	
Prince Berthold	Alice Little
Claimant of the Duchy.	
Melchior	Jennie Tuttle
His Confidant.	
Sabyne	Elsie Hammond
Adolf	Clare Allen
Her Attendants.	

PLACE: The Palace at Juliers.   TIME: 16—

ACT I.   An Ante-chamber.
ACT II.   The Presence-chamber.
ACT III.--ACT IV.   Same as Act I.
ACT V.   The Presence-chamber.

Presented by the Senior Class
Mount Holyoke College
Tuesday, May twenty-seventh
Nineteen Hundred Two

Fanny Perkins was interested not only in acting—she played Gaucelme in the senior class production of Colombe's Birthday—but also in writing. After graduation, using a pseudonym, she submitted a number of love stories for publication in women's magazines.

Her grades were never impressive, although they did improve somewhat as she approached graduation.

In terms of her future career, the most important course that she took at Mount Holyoke was not in her major. During her senior year she studied American economic history with Professor Annah May Soule. As part of the course requirements, Professor Soule required her students to visit the factories in the neighboring town of Holyoke and to write summaries of the working conditions they personally witnessed there. The dirt, the poor lighting, and the dangerous working conditions she observed first-hand in these Holyoke factories began her transformation from an unconcerned student to a passionate advocate of industrial reform. Thinking back a half-century later on the impact that course and its professor had on her, Perkins recalled, "I think she... opened the door to the idea that... the lack of comfort and security in some people was not solely due to the fact that they drank, which had been the prevailing view in my parental society...."

Annah May Soule, a history professor at Mount Holyoke, introduced Perkins to the idea that poverty was not necessarily the result of immorality.

Perkins's parents, who were very involved in the Congregational Church, had always been charitable people, helping out needy neighbors with rent money, old clothes, and part-time jobs in Mr. Perkins's store. But they basically believed that poverty was caused by laziness or liquor. Her visits to factories taught their daughter, however, that poverty could also result from industrial accidents, such as the loss of a hand in a malfunctioning machine.

Some of Professor Soule's students founded a local chapter of the National Consumers' League, an organization aimed at using consumer pressure to improve industrial conditions. At their invitation Florence Kelley, the executive secretary of the organization, came to speak at Mount Holyoke on February

20, 1902. Almost exactly 30 years later, Florence Kelley died, and at a memorial meeting in New York City a month later Perkins was among those who spoke. She recalled Kelley's willingly braving the rigors of winter travel in New England to address "a little handful of girls studying economics or sociology... to tell them about the program which she was evolving for industrial and human and social justice.... She took a whole group of young people, form-less in their aspirations, and molded their aspirations for social justice into some definite purpose, into a program that had meaning and that had experience and that had practicality back of it."

But it would still be a few years before Perkins's own budding interest in social justice would develop into a coherent career path. After she graduated from Mount Holyoke, she floundered about for a while. For unlike men graduating from college at the time, who could pre-pare for careers in public service by studying law or going into business, there was no comparable route for women with similar educations and aspirations. Perkins and other college-educated women of her generation gained politi-cal experience by doing whatever they could to advance such causes as the abolition of child labor and securing the vote for women. Only later, making use of the network they created among themselves and some supportive men, could they exercise political power on the state and national level.

Perkins had heard about the Charity Organization Society of New York, whose goal in the long term was to identify and eliminate the causes of poverty and, in the short term, to direct needy people to an appropriate chari-ty. Having learned the name of the director, she boldly made her way into his office, lacking both parental approval and an appointment. At the interview, Edward T. Devine politely but firmly told the determined but naive young woman that before she could be of help to others, she would have to gain some life experience. He encouraged her to prepare herself by teaching and reading.

Among the titles on the reading list he gave her was *How the Other Half Lives,* the 1890 exposé of the terrible conditions in the New York City slums by Danish-born American journalist and reformer Jacob Riis. That book's effect on her was considerable, as she wrote in her 1946 biography of Franklin Roosevelt: "I ... read it, ... and ... straightaway felt that the pursuit of social justice would be my vocation." Riis not only explained that the suffering of the "other half" affected those with more comfortable lives by leading to epidemics and crime, but he also challenged his readers: "What are you going to do about it? is the question of to-day."

Following Edward Devine's advice to find a teaching position, however, proved a bit more of a challenge than finding a book. During her first postgraduate semester she was able to find work only as a substitute teacher at an academy in Connecticut. Periodically, members of her Mount Holyoke class were asked to send in to the college an update on their activities, so that friends could keep abreast of each other's progress through life. In December 1902 she described in her first Mount Holyoke class letter the variety of courses she had found herself teaching: "Algebra and Geometry (think of that for this child), Physics, Zoology, Physical Geography, and Geology (bluff) and college English."

Perhaps more interesting to her than the teaching was an attempt to better the lives of working girls. Back at home in Worcester, she told her classmates, she was now running "a most interesting Girls' Club. Girls from 14 to 16 and most of them working in the factories and stores already. We meet twice a week now and on one night we have gymnasium work and gym games....they are all hollow-chested and never get any exercise after being cramped up all day."

She ran her Girls' Club on the premises of a Worcester settlement house—one of many establishments in underprivileged areas around the country that provided social services to local residents. The first settlement was founded in London in 1884 by Samuel Augustus Barnett, vicar of St. Jude's parish. Barnett invited graduates of Oxford and Cambridge universities to join him and his wife in "settling" in the deprived area by living in Toynbee Hall, named for the recently deceased social reformer Arnold Toynbee. There, Barnett hoped, they could learn about the neighborhood's social conditions and contribute to its life. The first settlement in the United States, modeled on Toynbee Hall, opened on the Lower East Side of New York City in 1886. The movement soon spread elsewhere in the country, and ultimately to most of the countries of western Europe, as well as to Southeast Asia and Japan.

Mary Hogan, one of Perkins's charges in the settlement house club, was a worker in a candy factory. In a grotesque accident Hogan's hand was chopped off in a candy dipper. Irate that the factory had simply sent Hogan home, Perkins first arranged for a doctor to visit her. Then, outraged to discover that the injured girl had no legal right to a cash award from the candy manufacturer, Perkins enlisted the aid of a clergyman, and the two managed to secure a single payment of $100 for Hogan.

After teaching for a semester at an academy in Worcester and for an academic year at another academy elsewhere in Massachusetts, Perkins found a more prestigious teaching position in Lake Forest, Illinois, a wealthy Chicago suburb. Hired to teach physics and biology and to serve as a dormitory head at Ferry Hall, a well-known boarding school for girls west of the Appalachians, she underwent significant personal changes during the three years she taught there. She heralded this transformation most obviously when in June 1905 she changed both her religion and her name. Fanny Coralie Perkins—raised in her parents' Congregational church—was confirmed and enrolled in the Episcopal church of Lake Forest as Frances C. Perkins. In December 1905 she registered in the guest book at Chicago Commons, a settlement house on the west side of Chicago, as Frances Perkins, and never used her middle initial again.

During her frequent vacation-time stays not only at Chicago Commons but also at Hull House, probably the most famous of all American settlement houses, Perkins was exposed to ideas at odds with those of her parents. When she arrived in Chicago, fresh from her charitable work in Worcester, she thought trade unions "were an evil to be avoided, if possible. You did good to the poor with charitable relief, friendly visiting,... mother's clubs, and that sort of thing...." But at Hull House she encountered both staff members and residents who believed that trade union organization was the answer to many of the problems of poverty. One Sunday afternoon, after she had helped run an entertainment for the neighborhood, she took her confusion about how to improve the lot of the poor to the son of the founder of Chicago Commons. The memory of the blond young man's emphatic conviction remained with her over the decades. Punctuating his statements with the pounding of a fist, he told her, "If every working man and woman would join a trade union then the wages would be sufficient to support people and then the families would be able to look after themselves and there would not be this necessity for these various services that go on through the charity societies, the settlements and so forth."

As an untrained worker at these settlement houses, Perkins also learned to use her wits to achieve what she and her colleagues at the settlement houses perceived as social justice. Among the tasks assigned her was to visit employers who withheld payment from workers, usually immigrants, simply because they felt they could get away with it, and convince them to pay up. "I began to see that there was a reason for this trade union organization. There was a strong group that would collect the money. The union would see that the wages were paid on time and paid when they were earned."

While teaching at Ferry Hall, Perkins continued to read books suggested to her by the director of the New York Charity Organization Society as well as other titles that also shed light on the conditions of the working classes. Soon she began to feel that she had now carried out Edward T. Devine's advice to gain some practical experience, to teach, and to read before looking for a job in social work. She wrote everyone she knew with any connection to charitable societies. From a college friend she learned of an organization back east that was just in the process of setting itself up. In the fall of 1907, following some time off for her Mount Holyoke fifth reunion and a trip to Italy with two friends from Chicago, she moved to Philadelphia. There she became executive secretary of the Philadelphia Research and Protective Association.

A group of socially concerned individuals had set up this organization with its cumbersome title to find out just what was happening to the large influx of young immigrant women arriving in Philadelphia both from Europe and from the American South. Suspicions were soon confirmed that these women were being met at the docks and railroad stations by unscrupulous men who then directed them to lodging houses that turned out to be brothels or to employment agencies that charged exorbitant fees for placing them in positions. Perkins's job was to conduct research to determine just what the facts of the situation were, and then, if exploitation was confirmed, to find ways to correct the problem.

When people later asked Frances Perkins how she had risen to the top in the field of social work, she would answer, only half in jest, that she had begun at the top. Although Perkins had no formal training in social work, she was able to gather the necessary facts with the aid of a black woman assistant whom she hired. As she wrote in a class letter to her fellow Mount Holyoke alumnae in December 1909, her position in Philadelphia led her into "some strange and thrilling experiences." The most frightening of these adventures took place one rainy night. Two men who preyed on immigrant women followed her home in the dark, increasing their pace as she began to walk more quickly. Afraid for her personal safety but remembering her father's advice about methods of self-protection, she made a rapid turn around a dark corner and let the men run into her open umbrella. Then, at the top of her lungs, she screamed the name of one of her pursuers. When people's heads began to appear in windows, Sam Smith and his colleague turned on their heels and ran.

Immediately Perkins informed the local police, who put her in touch with the Commissioner of Public Safety and the director of the Bureau of Licenses. With the aid of these officials, Sam Smith was put out of business, as were other individuals who ran corrupt employment agencies and lodging houses. Influenced by the report Perkins prepared on the status of the immigrant women arriving in Philadelphia, the city authorities eventually arranged to have police patrol the docks and railroad stations to provide some protection to the new arrivals. She also helped draw up specifications for the licensing of lodging houses.

From her work at the Philadelphia Research and Protective Association, Perkins gained much experience that would help her in the years to come. She began to understand that even if local officials were themselves corrupt men, who saw nothing wrong with personally benefiting from graft, they could be instrumental in bringing about social justice. She learned to be an effective public speaker. "I would be asked to speak at some conference on social progress in Philadelphia and told I could speak five minutes. I had to learn to say something in five minutes." She also concluded that women workers were more likely to be exploited than their male counterparts.

While in Philadelphia, Perkins also went back to school. At the University of Pennsylvania's Graduate School of Arts and Sciences she not only studied economics and sociology but so sufficiently impressed her economics professor, Simon N. Patten, that he arranged for a graduate-school fellowship for her the following year at Columbia University in New York.

And so, in September 1909, Frances Perkins moved to New York City. Although she was already 29 years old, she was not unique among her Mount Holyoke classmates in being a single woman in pursuit of a professional career. Half her classmates were still unmarried, and nearly half of them were working. Nor was she unique in finding New York an inspiring place to live. It was a particularly exciting time to live in the city, where other idealistic young women (and men) flocked from other parts of the country. Like Perkins, these newcomers to the city often had an interest in exceeding their parents' expectations for them. Determined to do more than be well bred, they devoted themselves to women's causes, including economic independence, birth control, and the suffrage movement. Many of these independent young women would form informal support networks that would help all of them advance their programs for social justice.

As Perkins reported to her classmates in the December 1909 class letter, she found time in New York City to enjoy the opera, theater, and dinners in picturesque cafes with a growing circle of men and women friends. But despite a busy social life she also felt herself "in the very heart of both the theoretical and practical efforts to socialize the life of the modern city." Reflecting on that time of her life more than 40 years later, Perkins commented, "I don't think people realize how much professional and cultural life women had if they wanted it before the days of woman suffrage."

As director of investigations for the New York State Factory Investigation Commission in 1911, Perkins showed reporters a ladder that served as the only fire escape for factory workers.

2

IF IT COULD BE DONE IN NEW YORK, IT COULD BE DONE ANYWHERE

A hot topic among Perkins's classmates, and other Americans, at the time she moved to New York was whether women should be granted the right to vote. Interestingly enough, Perkins's father, very conservative in other ways, was a strong supporter of the woman suffrage movement, and his enthusiasm inspired his daughter. He told her about asking an elderly worker at the Perkins family property in Maine what he thought of giving the vote to women. The man had answered that if the town fool, Jake Francis, could vote, it stood to reason that Perkins's educated and intelligent daughter Frances should be allowed to vote as well.

Perkins believed that only when women were able to vote would the social issues she felt deeply about receive the attention they merited. To achieve that end she was glad to be sent by the local leaders of the movement to give speeches in a variety of neighborhoods. She learned to take hecklers in stride, to project her voice over traffic noises, and to defuse a potentially explosive situation by telling a joke.

In her December 1909 update of her life for her classmates, however, Perkins made it clear that she knew not all Mount Holyoke alumnae shared her commitment to the suffrage movement. Suffrage for women, she wrote, "is either execrated so heartily or championed so ardently by all of you that it needs only the bare statement of the fact that I'm one of the 'real ones' to explain the situation perfectly."

Involved as she was in securing the vote for women (a goal finally achieved in New York in 1917 and throughout the United States as a whole in 1920), Perkins did not forget that what had brought her to New York was a research fellowship and the pursuit of an advanced degree. Her research project was to make a study of undernourished children attending Public School 51 in the New York neighborhood suggestively called Hell's Kitchen, which extended from 34th Street northward to 53rd Street and from Eighth Avenue westward to the Hudson River. She lived in Hell's Kitchen herself for a while as a resident of the local settlement, Hartley House.

Hell's Kitchen, like other New York neighborhoods at the time, was controlled by a "boss," known as the MacManus. Thomas J. MacManus was only one among many locally powerful Democratic political figures who were subordinates of the main boss, Charles Murphy. Murphy was the head of Tammany Hall, as the executive committee of the New York City Democratic party was called. An encounter with the MacManus while she was still at Hartley House reinforced Perkins's belief, instilled in her in Philadelphia, that although local political leaders might be corrupt, they could still be forces for good. A distraught woman with several dependent children came to Hartley House one day to say that her son, the sole support of the family, had been arrested. Perkins took it upon herself to go to the local office of the Charity Organization Society to see if they could do something for the family, but they said it would take them some time to study the matter.

Giving the mother a handout from her own pocket to tide her over, Perkins then took herself to the Ninth Avenue office of the MacManus and explained the situation to him. Overnight—she never asked what strings were pulled or what palms greased—the boy was released and was back at work to support the family.

In addition to her field work among the schoolchildren and her community work through Hartley House, Perkins also took economics and sociology courses at Columbia. One course, "Misery and Its Causes," was taught by Edward T. Devine, whom she had first met seven years earlier when she was a newly minted college graduate. On June 10, 1910, Columbia awarded Perkins—now 30 years old—a master's degree in political science. A revised version of her master's thesis, "Some Facts Concerning Certain Undernourished Children," appeared in the October 10, 1910, issue of *The Survey*, a professional journal read by settlement workers and other social workers. Perkins's conclusion sounded a note that would become a recurring theme associated with her: "Temporary relief is necessary, and its method may well deserve discussion, but it is after all only an expedient to head off malnutrition until society adjusts itself and provides adequate incomes and adequate education to all its workers."

Despite the demands of school and settlement, Perkins somehow managed to find time for a busy social life in New York. At a late-afternoon tea dance in 1910 at the home of Mrs. Walston Brown in Gramercy Park, she made the acquaintance of a tall, thin young man named Franklin Roosevelt. She might not have remembered the encounter except for his words in support of the policies of Theodore Roosevelt, to whom he was distantly related, and whose Presidential politics both he and Perkins admired.

Even before she had finished her degree she was hired as executive secretary, or chief executive officer, of the New York Consumers' League, the local branch of the National

Consumers' League. She found herself now not only a junior colleague of Florence Kelley, whose address one wintry night at Mount Holyoke had helped direct Perkins's career path, but also with an office near Edward T. Devine's in the Charities Building.

In her new position Perkins came to believe that whatever trade unions might accomplish, new laws could be of much wider social value, and that the Consumers' League and other organizations like it could help secure their passage. As chief officer of the New York Consumers' League for a little more than two years she was in charge of lobbying for and securing passage of a major piece of legislation, the 54-Hour Bill, which prohibited women of any age and boys under 18 from working in factories more than 54 hours per week. She also administered two major studies— of the sanitary conditions in the 2,500 New York City bakeries that operated out of cellars, and of fire prevention techniques in factories.

To collect data for her first study Perkins visited more than 100 cellar bakeries. Discovering cats sleeping and giving birth on breadboards and tubercular children coughing into bread dough, she uncovered the horrifying conditions in which New Yorkers' bread was prepared. Then a factory fire on November 26, 1910, in nearby Newark, New Jersey, led to her next study. Alarmed by a warning from the New York City fire chief that many of the city's factories were no better equipped with fire exits than the factory in Newark had been, Perkins set about gathering information.

With both studies under way, in January 1911 Perkins first went to Albany, the seat of New York State government, to begin her initial lobbying efforts on behalf of the Consumers' League's 54-Hour Bill. There she first met two influential Democrats whose careers would intertwine with hers for many years to come: assemblyman Alfred E. Smith and state senator Robert F. Wagner. Although she was

SOME FACTS CONCERNING CERTAIN UNDERNOURISHED CHILDREN

This article, Perkins's first published article in the field of social work, is a short-ened version of her Columbia University master's thesis. It appeared in the October 10, 1910, edition of The Survey, *a journal read by settlement workers and other community leaders. In the article, Perkins argues that malnutrition in children is often a symptom of larger social ills affecting the child and its family.*

No one today denies that in every large city in the United States there are many school children who are habitually undernourished, nor does any thinking person deny that this malnutrition results in susceptibility to disease, in inability to study, and in general inefficiency.

The question discussed at present is how to prevent malnutrition and relieve a situation which is felt to be intolerable, but the causes of which are so closely bound up with a variety of social ills that it is diffi-cult to separate them distinctly. While a case of malnutrition is obvious to a physician, the elements in the daily life of the child which con-tribute to bring about this state are seldom well understood. The study here presented was made in an attempt to understand the family and social circumstances of a definite though small number of children who were obviously the victims of malnutrition.

The opportunity to make such an investigation arose in connection with an experiment in feeding undernourished children, conducted by the School Lunch Committee in February, 1910. The selection of the 107 children who were the subjects of this study was made by a Board of Health physician in a public school on the upper West Side of New York city. The doctor examined all the children in the four lower grades

text continues on page 28

text continued from page 27

and selected those who were evidently suffering from malnutrition. The 107 cases so selected were thirteen per cent of all the children in those grades.

Poor teeth are the commonest physical defect recorded. The great predominance of such non-nutritive foods as coffee or tea and bread in the diet of most of these children, and the almost universal habit of soaking the bread until it is soft, can hardly have failed to have some deteriorating effect on the teeth. Dental experts, too, agree that where the teeth become bad, whether from lack of care or lack of proper food, they are likely to bring about all sorts of digestive disorders. Thus, while defective teeth serve to aggravate malnutrition already established, it is equally true that undernourishment may have been the cause of the poor teeth....

The families from which these undernourished children came...[as] a whole...were intelligent and self-reliant. Only five families had ever asked for aid from the Charity Organization Society or the Association for Improving the Condition of the Poor, and in only five were there cases of marked intemperance.

For the most part the size of the families was normal.... The tenements of this district do not offer desirable homes to families of any income.... Sleeping in dark, ill-ventilated rooms, as so many of these children do, can but add to their malnutrition, as the normal supply of oxygen from the air is cut off....

unsuccessful in her attempts to have the bill passed that year, 1911 was hardly an uneventful one for her.

On Saturday afternoon, March 25, 1911, Perkins was at a small tea party at the home of Mrs. Gordon Norrie in New York's Washington Square. All of a sudden the guests were distracted by fire engine sirens and the sound of screaming. She later recalled, "Without saying much of anything, we all went down the steps and just went toward the fire. It was just about that time that they began to jump. It was the most horrible sight." Purely by chance Perkins was a witness to the historic fire at the Triangle Shirtwaist Company, where women's tailored blouses were manufactured.

The fire broke out on the eighth floor of the Asch Building, just east of Washington Square Park, and quickly spread upward to the two top floors of the building. The building's overloaded fire escape soon collapsed, and most of the people who survived got out of the building by elevator. Although the building had two elevators, one broke down after only a few trips. It later turned out that the elevator had not been inspected for many months, in violation of the law. A single stairway that could have provided an exit to other workers was locked. The management had been determined not only to prevent union organizers from entering the building but also to prevent workers from passing goods out of the building to real or imagined thieving accomplices. Seeing no other way out of the building, many workers jumped out the windows to their deaths. In all, 146 people died in the fire, mostly young immigrant women.

The city was stunned by the disaster. As Perkins later recalled, "These were the days when nobody expected the government to do anything. The citizens voluntarily came together...to devise preventive methods, and to insist upon their being carried out...they certainly embraced the idea that there might be a law which could be properly enforced which would prevent this type of disaster." On Sunday, April 2, 1911, Perkins was one of 350 citizens who gathered in New York City's Metropolitan Opera House. Although there were many speeches, years later Perkins could remember clearly only the words of tiny, red-haired Rose Schneiderman, a leader of the Shirtwaist Makers Union: "This is not the first time girls have been burned alive in this city.... Every year thousands of us are maimed. The life of men and women is so cheap and property is so sacred! There are so many of us for one job, it matters little if 140-odd are burned to death.... I can't talk fellowship to you who are gathered here. Too much blood has been spilled. I know from experience it is up to the working people to save themselves. And the only way is through a strong working-class movement."

Moved as she was by Schneiderman's chilling words, Perkins disagreed with her in one respect. Although Perkins had by now come to believe that trade unions were valuable, she believed that organizations like the Consumers' League could do much to improve the working conditions of laboring men and women.

Following various protest meetings, a number of New York City civic leaders organized a Committee on Safety. Since Perkins had been doing research for the Consumers' League on the hazards of factory fires, she was called upon to share her knowledge with the Committee on Safety and was put on a committee to urge the governor of New York to take some action. She thus came into contact with other public-spirited New Yorkers, including some of its wealthiest citizens and most important professional leaders. The bonds among these reform-minded New Yorkers remained firm over the years.

In response to the public demand, the state legislature appointed the New York State Factory Investigating Commission, effective June 30, 1911, with broad powers to study not only factory fires but also sanitation, industrial disease, and other safety and health issues. State Senator Wagner was named chairman of the Factory Investigating Commission, and Assemblyman Al Smith was named vice-chairman. The commission included a second state senator, two other assemblymen, and four members of the public. Although Perkins was not herself a member of the commission, she later recalled that "I did know a great deal about the subject. I was one of the few people who knew anything about factories. I was constantly being called as a witness about fire, about accident, about sanitation, about various things. Finally I became an investigator for them and then I became kind of in charge of investigations."

As director of investigations for the commission, Perkins made it her business to educate its members. She made sure that Al Smith personally witnessed the physical exhaustion of women leaving their twelve-hour night shift at the rope works in Auburn, New York, and that Robert Wagner personally experienced the inadequacy of many factory fire escapes by having him crawl through a tiny hole in the wall and down an icy iron ladder that ended 12 feet from the ground. On another occasion she organized an early morning trip with the members of the commission to an upstate canning factory, where they saw children as young as five preparing vegetables. Perkins later summarized the effect on the commission members of the expeditions she organized for them: "Alfred Smith said it was the greatest education he'd ever had. He had no idea life was like that. He'd grown up in the slums of New York, but he did not know what factory life was like. Neither did any of them. It was an astonishment for them to see the frightfully filthy conditions, the obvious fire hazards and the very great accident hazards."

The year 1911 was a watershed not only in Perkins's professional life but in her personal life also. By the summer of that year she was receiving love letters from Paul C. Wilson, an economist four years her senior. A graduate of

In 1918, about five years after this photograph was taken, Paul Wilson, Perkins's husband, fell victim to what would probably be diagnosed today as bipolar disorder.

the University of Chicago, Wilson had come to New York in 1906 with his close friend and fellow economist Henry Bruère, to join the staff of the Bureau of Municipal Research, a private fact-finding agency that hoped to reform city government through scientific study. Much of the bureau's work at that time was directed toward improving the city's financial methods. A 1933 profile of Perkins in *The New Yorker* described Wilson as "one of the most civilized and intelligent men on Manhattan Island." Perkins had already laughed off the marriage proposal of at least one famous suitor—the author Sinclair Lewis, who in 1930 became the first American awarded the Nobel Prize for literature for his novels, including *Babbitt, Arrowsmith, Elmer Gantry,* and *Dodsworth.* Although the two had been good friends and remained on friendly terms, the relationship was not a serious romantic one for either Perkins or Lewis.

The following year, with the help of her friend from Hell's Kitchen, the MacManus, and another powerful Tammany leader, Big Tim Sullivan, "King of the Bowery," Perkins succeeded in bringing about the passage of the 54-Hour Bill. The bill, which she had championed since 1910, when she first was hired by the New York Consumer's

League, did not pass, however, without Perkins's eyes being opened to the political tricks played by other members of the legislature. At the last minute she had to make a decision that she feared would bring upon her the wrath of Florence Kelley, the executive secretary of the National Consumers' League, whom she had admired since her senior year in college. Rather than see the bill go down to defeat another time, Perkins agreed to accept a version that covered the 400,000 women factory workers in New York State except for the 10,000 in the canning industry.

The following morning she met with Mrs. Kelley, expecting to be admonished. Instead, as Perkins later told a reporter for *The New Yorker,* Mrs. Kelley joyously exclaimed, "'Frances, Frances, we have won; you have done it!'... and threw her arms around my neck and cried." With Perkins in place as a lobbyist in Albany, Kelley's growing network of women reformers had achieved a long-desired goal. To the delight of the bill's advocates, the following year the legislators extended the scope of the 54-Hour Law to include the canneries.

Franklin Roosevelt was a state senator in 1912 when the debate over the 54-Hour Bill took place. Remembering him as an admirer of reform-minded President Theodore Roosevelt, Perkins had hoped the younger Roosevelt would join her in supporting the bill. In *The Roosevelt I Knew,* Perkins commented on her disappointment at his lack of involvement in the struggle: "Franklin Roosevelt did not associate himself actively with this bill....I took it hard that a young man who had so much spirit did not do so well in this, which I thought a test, as did Tim Sullivan and the MacManus, undoubtedly corrupt politicians."

In May 1912, the month following the signing of the 54-Hour Bill, Perkins left her position at the New York Consumers' League to become the chief officer of the Committee on Safety. Perkins now became actively involved in writing up legislation for Smith and Wagner and the other legislators on the Factory Investigating Commission to introduce to the legislature. Recalling the yellow pads on which she drafted legislation in pencil, Perkins later described how, together with her friend and colleague Bernard Shientag, then assistant counsel to the commission, "I wrote with [my] own hands most of the New York State labor law that was finally passed."

The interaction between the Factory Investigating Commission and the Committee on Safety resulted eventually in the passage of 36 new state laws to protect industrial workers. Perkins was aware that other states were also passing new labor laws, but she believed these achievements, though encouraging, were not truly significant. In *The Roosevelt I Knew* she underscored the greater influence of progressive legislation passed in the nation's industrial powerhouse state: "New York! If it could be done there, it could be done anywhere."

In that book Perkins also recalled an experience she had when paying a call on Charles Murphy, the boss of Tammany Hall, to enlist his support for bills on factory buildings then being deliberated in the state legislature. Having heard her say her piece, Murphy sat forward in his chair and quietly asked, "You are the young lady, aren't you, who managed to get the fifty-four-hour bill passed?"

When she owned up to that fact, he admitted that though he had not supported that bill, he had since observed that voters had responded to its passage by supporting Democratic candidates. He promised to tell his "boys" to give her whatever help they could to smooth the passage of her new bills. As she began to leave Murphy's office, he caught her off guard by inquiring if she was "one of these women suffragists." Worried that she might alienate his support if she acknowledged she was, she nonetheless decided to tell the truth. Murphy then closed their interview by saying that though he personally did not support suffrage for women, "if anybody ever gives them the vote, I hope you will remember that you would make a good Democrat."

Two events that would have long-term consequences for Perkins took place in 1913. The first occurred on March 4, when the U.S. Department of Labor was established. As executive secretary of the New York Consumers' League, Perkins had been among the agency heads putting pressure on the government to create such a department. Although she would have some contact with the Department of Labor over the next two decades, she was disappointed that it seemed to do so little. Little did she imagine at the time that exactly 20 years later she would become that department's chief official.

The second event of the year whose effects would reverberate through her life took place on September 26, when Frances Perkins was married to Paul C. Wilson in an Episcopal church ceremony in New York City. Perkins, now 33, and Wilson, 37, were both intensely private individuals, and they invited neither family nor friends to the wedding.

Dressing alone in her apartment for the wedding, Perkins was surprised to receive a call from the wife and the mother of the principal proprietor of the Triangle Shirtwaist Company, who was then being brought to trial. The women beseeched her to ask for clemency on his behalf, saying that he was a good husband and father, that he had meant no harm. With no one around whose advice she could ask, Perkins finally told the women she would not intervene. Their loved one's life and personal happiness were less significant than making the public understand the tragic consequences of his failure to observe the law.

Perkins later claimed that she had not been particularly eager to marry but that she finally decided to so that people would stop challenging her about her reluctance. But marrying did not mean giving up her personal identity, and she described two reasons why she insisted on keeping her family name. First, she had by this time developed a reputation in her field, and she was loath to lose the name recognition and to have people dismissing her as simply someone's wife. "I suppose I had been somewhat touched by feminist ideas and that was one of the reasons I kept my maiden name. My whole generation was, I suppose, the first generation that openly and actively asserted—at least some of us did—the separateness of women and their personal independence in the family relationship."

Perkins's second reason for maintaining her own last name had to do with the potential conflict between her own professional life and Wilson's. At the time of their marriage, Wilson was actively involved in New York City's campaign for mayor. His candidate was John Purroy Mitchel, no friend of Tammany Hall, who promised to reform city government. In November 1913, Mitchel won the mayoralty of New York and appointed Wilson assistant secretary to the mayor, to assist him with budgetary decisions and other matters concerning the expenditure of city funds. Perkins worried that her own professional activities might have a negative impact on Wilson's: "After my husband became a part of the Mitchel administration I had another very firm reason for it, which was that by using his name every time I made a wild speech in Buffalo about fire hazards in New York City it might be an embarrassment to the Mitchel administration. I would have had the feeling that I ought to shut up for fear of hurting him. But Miss Frances Perkins, rising in Buffalo, talking about the fire hazards in the City of New York, that didn't hurt anybody."

She never made a fuss, however, when her mother introduced her to friends as Mrs. Wilson, and always signed hotel registries when checking in with her husband as "Mr. and Mrs. Paul C. Wilson." Somewhat surprisingly, Perkins insisted, "I'm a conformist whatever else I am."

Whatever professional barrier Perkins decided to raise between her own job and her husband's, an economic initiative undertaken by the Mitchel administration in 1914 was to influence her future thinking. By late 1914 there was a serious economic downturn in the industrial areas of the United States. Many unemployed workers, dubbing themselves (for reasons historians do not know) "the ginks," poured into New York City. Wilson's friend Henry Bruère, now chamberlain of the city in Mayor Mitchel's administration, was put in charge of the unemployment problem. The city took over an empty old loft building on the Bowery and, after minor renovations, opened it up as a shelter. Neither the Hotel de Gink, as it came to be known, nor the various work programs that Bruère tried to institute solved the problem of unemployment, but Perkins was impressed by the attempts to provide relief. After the crisis passed she participated in a minor way in preparing Bruère's 1918 report providing recommendations for dealing with periodic unemployment. Observing Bruère put his different programs into effect, Perkins later recalled, "was the first contact I ever had directly with mass unemployment."

In February 1915 the Factory Investigating Commission submitted its final report to the legislature, and the work of the Committee on Safety began to wind down. Perkins, now pregnant, had every intention of finishing up her work for the committee and then becoming "more and more of a domestic person, writing and lecturing on these subjects, keeping up my expert standing, but serving as committee member, adviser, and so forth." When the baby born that spring died shortly thereafter, Perkins became very ill and spent several months in bed. She kept her feelings about the loss very much to herself, and few friends from later periods in her life were even aware of it. She seems to have dealt with her grief by throwing herself into her work. From her bed she finished drafting legislation, contacting various experts by telephone.

The following year began with another death and ended with a birth. In February 1916, Fred Perkins, the father whom she remembered as "the sweetest looking person," died. On December 30, Perkins gave birth to a healthy daughter, Susanna Winslow Wilson, named for an ancestor on her mother's side, the wife of the second governor of the Plymouth colony. Perkins hired a nurse to help her care for the baby while she finished up her work at the Committee on Safety.

On April 19, 1917, the United States entered World War I, which had begun in Europe on July 28, 1914, and war work occupied many of Perkins's colleagues until the hostilities were ended on November 11, 1918. Perkins herself accepted the position of executive secretary of the New York Council of Women for War Work, an agency created to match qualified women with appropriate positions to aid

Soon after Susanna Winslow Wilson was born in 1916, Perkins found that the experience of being a working mother gave her a new understanding of the experiences of other working women.

the war effort. Half a year later, the November 1917 elections caused both disappointment and elation in the Perkins-Wilson household. While John Purroy Mitchel's second mayoral campaign went down to defeat, women were granted suffrage in New York State.

In 1918 Perkins began to put into effect her plan to curtail her professional commitments and to spend more time at home. She hoped to have at least one more child. Drawing on her experience as a mother who had lost a baby and survived a serious complication after childbirth, she agreed to serve as the unsalaried executive secretary of the Maternity Center Association, a national voluntary group dedicated to reducing infant mortality and the high death rates of mothers.

But what Perkins later dismissed as "one of the accidents of life" occurred in mid-1918 and forced her to rethink her plans. Wilson became ill sometime in 1918, and her life would never be the same again. "My husband suffered from an up and down illness all the way through. It was always up and down. He was sometimes depressed, sometimes excited.... From 1918 on there were never anything but very short periods of reasonably comfortable accommodations to life.... Sometimes he was hospitalized, sometimes not. Sometimes he would go off on a little trip. Sometimes he would have an attendant that was called a secretary. There was great variety in the whole process."

Wilson had inherited what Perkins called "a very sizable fortune." That money and their individual earnings had enabled them to live very nicely in New York. As she wrote her classmates in their fourth class letter in 1915, their house at 121 Washington Place was "comfortable, though old fashioned, and there always appear to be plenty of competent professional household workers who want to take care of the house and me and my man." In addition, they had a weekend house "on the edge of Long Island Sound." Now, however, Wilson lost a great deal of money by speculating in gold stocks. "Part of the illness, really, had to do with the exaggerated use of money." Perkins, at age 38, realized that from now on she would have to support herself, her ill husband, and their child.

Little did she anticipate when she involved herself in the 1918 gubernatorial campaign of Al Smith, her friend and colleague from the Factory Investigating Commission days, that she would find in his administration the job she not only needed but was also most highly suited for. But in early January 1919, Governor Al Smith summoned her to Albany and asked her to be a member of the Industrial Commission of the New York State Department of Labor. When she asked him to explain why he wanted her of all people, Smith gave her several reasons: from her work investigating factory conditions she knew as well as he did

In 1919 Perkins, topped off as usual with a hat wider than her cheekbones, was appointed by the new New York State governor, Al Smith, to join the Industrial Commission of the state's Department of Labor. The appointment gave her both the income she needed and a platform from which she could help other people.

how badly the Industrial Commission needed reform; he believed it was the right thing to do to bring a qualified woman into state government now that women had the vote; and he had from their first meetings been impressed by her ability to speak clearly.

After some thought, Perkins agreed to accept the job. On her return to New York City she sought out Florence Kelley to ask her blessing. To Perkins's delight, the emotional Mrs. Kelley "burst into tears and she said exactly what Al Smith had said she would say—'Glory be to God. You don't mean it. I never thought I would live to see the day when someone that we had trained and whom we knew knew industrial conditions, cared about women, cared to have things right would have the chance to be the administrative officer.'" The appointment was announced on January 15, 1919. The fact that with a salary of $8,000 a year (about $90,000 in 1998) she would be one of the most highly paid women ever to serve in state government would certainly help Perkins face the challenges that lay ahead.

3

CONSTANT PROGRESS

Not everyone was delighted with Governor Al Smith's choice of Frances Perkins to fill a vacant seat in the New York State Industrial Commission. Both manufacturers and laborers claimed the seat should by rights go to one of their people. Some men were outraged that a woman should have such a lofty government position.

According to the *Mount Holyoke Alumnae Quarterly* of April 1919, Governor Smith responded to the protest by saying, "I appointed Miss Perkins because of her ability and her knowledge of the department of labor and the statutes affecting labor. She was very active in the legislative investigation that resulted in the labor code." Smith went on to say that it was appropriate in a state where millions of women were employed to have a woman on the industrial commission. "Having settled the question of appointing a woman, I could think of no one better fitted by knowledge and ability than Miss Perkins."

The same article also quotes Smith as saying, "To be honest, I do not know whether she is a democrat or a republican." But sometime after February 18, 1919, when the New York State Senate confirmed Perkins's appoint-

*In a rare view of Frances Perkins's private life, she, her husband, her daughter Susanna, and a friend
march in their own Fourth of July parade.*

ment by a vote of 34 to 16, at Smith's insistence she finally registered as a Democrat. She remarked decades later, "I know Republicanism because I was brought up in New England when it was fully Republican and when everybody I knew, all my family, were all Republican." But she now made herself a member of the Democratic family, whose commitment to help correct social wrongs through government intervention she had admired for some time.

Perkins herself was a bit worried about how welcome her appointment would be to John Mitchell, the former head of the United Mine Workers and now the chairman of the Industrial Commission, and the other three members of the commission. Among the harshest testimony Perkins had delivered to the Factory Investigating Commission was a sharp critique of the Industrial Commission run by these very men. She had publicly blamed them for allowing a fire to take place in a small candy factory in Brooklyn by failing to put into place the Factory Investigating Commission's recommendations. She had signed her name at the top of a petition to the governor to remove them all. As she later recalled, "I couldn't believe that I would be received with any very hearty enthusiasm."

A friend and associate from the Factory Investigating Commission advised her not to act embarrassed around her new colleagues. "Just go in boldly," he told her. "Smile as though nothing had happened. Be polite to everybody. After all, they're all politicians." That she managed in a short time both to shake up the Industrial Commission and to win the respect of the other four commissioners she later attributed to her "easy-going" personality.

Her first days on the job were, indeed, a bit uncomfortable. None of the commissioners had sent her any word of welcome or attempted to provide her with any orientation or guidance. She knew that the Industrial Commission consisted of two major divisions, a Factory Investigation Division and a Workmen's Compensation Division. By asking a few questions she soon learned that the former division was almost totally neglected in favor of the latter. She assumed that the commissioners preferred the good feeling that comes from making "an award to a workman who has obviously been hurt" to the hard work in determining "how wide the stairs [in a factory building] should be, whether there's been a compliance with this law or not."

Within a short time she had fostered a good relationship with the commission's chairman, John Mitchell. By asking his advice before undertaking any action on her own, she won him over. In the summer of 1919 the relationship between them played a crucial role in their success in settling what might otherwise have been a very violent strike in the copper works at Rome, New York, in Oneida County.

The copper workers' strike that broke out there in June 1919 was only one of many conflicts between labor and management in the period immediately following World War I. As Perkins later recalled, the copper workers felt abused. "They didn't get their wages raised. They were earning less than anybody in the United States doing the same kind of work. The hours had been lengthened without any compensatory pay....They knew at the same time that their employers had made fortunes. They could see the evidences of the fortunes in the fine new houses and snappy automobiles which they were driving around." The workers tried sending delegations of representatives to the employers, but the employers refused to meet with them. One employer, James A. Spargo, was particularly rough with the workers' representatives, throwing them downstairs from his office, directing foul language at them, and shooting a gun wildly into a crowd of workers. After workers attacked Spargo on July 14, 1919, Smith sent Perkins on an overnight train to Rome to investigate the situation. The train's conductor, fearing for her safety, was reluctant to let her disembark, but she prevailed.

She learned that the mayor had convinced Governor Smith to call in the state police to restore order. One of the metal polishers confided in her that if the state police were not withdrawn, the workers would explode a stash of dynamite they had hidden. Perkins decided on her own that she would have to persuade Smith to withdraw the police without telling him about the dynamite. She feared that the more people who knew about the dynamite, the greater the likelihood of its being set off. Heeding her advice, Smith ordered the police to withdraw, though they remained on call in nearby Oneida.

On the night the police left town, her metal polisher informant took Perkins to the homes of two workers. He told the occupants that he had promised the lady to get rid of the dynamite if the governor got rid of the police. She watched with amazement and gratitude as the men descended into the cellars, bringing up dynamite in sacks, suitcases—even a baby carriage—and dumped their haul into the canal.

But even if a literally explosive situation had been averted, the strike still remained to be settled. Spargo himself had left town, leaving the situation in the hands of the other employers and the strikers. But before disappearing, Spargo had intensified the strikers' anger by sending a messenger to his workers bearing a letter dripping in obscenities. If the letter had been sent through the postal service, he would have been liable for imprisonment on charges of sending obscenity through the mail. The workers had entrusted the letter to Perkins.

Perkins decided to ask her fellow commissioners to come to Rome to hold a public hearing. In early August she was joined by her chairman, John Mitchell, and other colleagues who were available. Perkins had shown Spargo's letter to the other two commissioners, who found it deeply offensive. Keeping in mind both the intense heat of the summer and the fact that people in Rome ate dinner early, they called the hearing in the courthouse for six o'clock. Perkins later recalled, "They came together. The hall was crowded. Everybody in town was there.... Every window was crowded with eager faces looking at us. The balcony, all the galleries—everything was full. The steps of the court house were full. The park was full of people."

The commissioners began by having the workers not only repeat the lowest level of wages they would accept but also describe how they felt abused and humiliated by their employers. Next it was the employers' turn to express their side, which they said they would do only through their lawyers. The lawyers proceeded to say that the employers could not afford to pay the level of wages being demanded. They also stated categorically that they would not recognize any workers' union.

The hours were passing in the overheated courtroom. As 10:00 p.m. approached, Perkins decided it was time to play her trump card. She took Spargo's abusive letter from her purse and whispered to Mitchell that he would have to read it aloud to make clear to the other employers just why the workers felt so humiliated and resentful. Mitchell reluctantly agreed.

Perkins later recalled how Mitchell, his face drained of color, rose and cleared his throat. Addressing the packed courtroom, he explained that it was his painful duty to read aloud the communication from Spargo, but before doing so he would like to say a few words. Mitchell then made this moving speech: "These are workmen. These are human beings. God made them. They live here. They work here. They must be treated like human beings and when they are not the resentments that gather are terrible indeed. Because they have been so insulted they are so insistent upon having what they believe to be right and justice and having it guaranteed by the State Industrial Commission."

Clearing his throat a second time, he unfolded the letter to begin reading it. Before he could do so, one of the other employers leaped out of his seat to prevent Mitchell from revealing the letter's contents. "I want you to know, Mr. Chairman," he said, that none of the other employers "would ever have written such a letter." Although they agreed with Spargo about refusing to negotiate or to increase wages above an additional two cents per hour, they refused to share the blame for Spargo's foul letter, for which they condemned him publicly.

The audience spontaneously broke out into applause. Murmurs of approval of this employer's words spread through the courthouse. Before anyone knew what had happened, the employer pledged to reach an agreement with his workers by the next noon, if only Mitchell would adjourn the meeting immediately and refrain from reading the letter.

That night Perkins spoke to Smith, reporting that the strike was for all intents and purposes settled, but that he should not make any announcements yet. The following day the employers agreed to match the wages paid to copper and brass workers in Connecticut, the nearest competition.

On her way back to New York City, Perkins stopped in Albany to see Governor Smith. She thrilled him with the details of her experience, not sparing him the story about the dynamite. She recalled his telling her, "You sure had your nerve with you. It was a risky business all right. But now it's all over and I congratulate you, Commissioner."

In his autobiography, *Up to Now,* Smith himself looked back on this incident. He remembered how, when he sent Perkins as his representative to Rome, "The heads of the business were shocked to find that I had selected a woman to negotiate a treaty of peace between the workers and their employers. They seemed to imply by their attitude the belief that any such undertaking was entirely outside the province of a woman. Afterward the attorney [for the Rome Brass and Copper Company] told me that they wondered what was the matter with me that I would make any such suggestion, but after Frances Perkins had visited the city of Rome and called the warring sections into conference, one of the leading officials of the Rome Brass and Copper Company said to the attorney, 'Do us a favor and ask the Governor where he found that woman.'"

Shortly after going to work for Smith, "that woman" began to dress in a low-key, tasteful but unobtrusive manner that she never deviated from during the remaining decades of her professional life. On the theory that men responded best to powerful women when they reminded them of their mothers, Perkins avoided fashionable and colorful clothing in favor of a wardrobe of simple black dresses. In the one fashion statement she allowed herself, she nearly always complemented her business dress with a tricorn hat of the kind her mother had advised her to wear so many years before. The tricorn hat became not only a Perkins trademark but also an inspiration for the political cartoonists who began to comment on her career in newspapers and magazines.

Looking resolute, tasteful, and a bit more glamorous than usual, Perkins posed for a photograph in the mid-1920s.

During the rest of Smith's first term as governor (he was to serve four terms in all), Perkins helped correct corrupt practices in the workmen's compensation division of the Industrial Commission. Sometimes the employers and their insurance companies would persuade workers to sign agreements for a quick settlement without informing the injured workers that they were entitled to collect further money for permanent partial disabilities. Sometimes the insurance companies unreasonably delayed compensation payments, thus earning interest on the money withheld, at the expense of the injured worker. Perkins also helped establish conferences of the different referees in the work-men's compensation division to avoid big discrepancies in the way the law was applied and interpreted. To revitalize the Factory Investigation Division of the Industrial Commission, she arranged weekly meetings with the head of that division, who appeared before the commissioners to report on the status of his investigations. She also arranged for meetings of factory inspectors throughout the state.

In the elections of November 1920, Republicans won not only the White House but also the governor's mansion in New York. Nathan L. Miller defeated Smith, and from January 1921 through December 1922 Perkins had to find employment in the private sector. During that period she served as executive secretary of the Council on Immigrant Education, a project set up by a group of businessmen who wanted to help new immigrants adjust to and participate in the life of New York City. Her main task was to increase the availability and improve the quality of night-school teaching for the city's newest arrivals.

During Smith's period out of office, another Democrat suffered a blow much more severe than losing an election. Franklin D. Roosevelt, who had been the party's nominee for Vice President in the election of 1920 and whose candidacy had been officially seconded in a speech by Al Smith, fell victim to polio. In her biography of Roosevelt, Perkins described how his terrible experience humanized this wealthy and privileged man and made him understand the problems of the common person in a way he never had before. "Having been to the depths of trouble, he understood the problems of people in trouble." During the period of recuperation, Roosevelt's wife, Eleanor, who belonged to the Consumers' League and other organizations where her path had crossed Perkins's, took it upon herself to introduce him to labor leaders, including Rose Schneiderman of the Shirtwaist Makers Union. In this way, Perkins wrote, "the years of illness were constructive years for him."

THE FACTORY INSPECTOR

Perkins contributed an entry to the 1920 edition of the book Careers for Women, *edited by Catherine Filene, the director of the Intercollegiate Vocational Guidance Association. A veteran of the New York State Factory Investigating Commission, Perkins was a member of the Industrial Commission of the New York State Department of Labor at the time of the book's publication. The following excerpt from her entry (reprinted with the permission of Houghton Mifflin Company) explains the diverse skills and attributes required of a factory inspector, a job that Perkins valued highly.*

A factory inspector should have excellent health and a robust physique. Some athletic ability is highly desirable, for some of the inspections which women will be called upon to undertake involve considerable physical stamina, balance, poise, etc. She should have a bearing which is both courteous and authoritative, with sufficient strength of character and dignity to gain the respect and confidence of the employers and employees in the community in which she works.

A factory inspector must be a person of tact, otherwise by irritating persons with whom she comes in contact, she may involve the department which she represents in long and tedious prosecutions in order to secure compliance with the law. The best inspector is one who can secure compliance with the law without prosecutions.

She must be a person capable of making decisions, for upon her judgment and her reports will rest many of the most important acts of the department. She must be the type of person who is a quick and accurate observer and an equally accurate reporter of facts.

....Nothing is such drudgery to the educated and intelligent woman as to do work which is insignificant in its meaning. Factory inspection is of vast importance, not only to the people who work in the factories, but to the entire community, and such work well done may be looked upon as service to one's country....

In the election of 1922 Perkins campaigned for Smith, who won back the governorship of New York. She later recalled, "It wasn't assumed that the minute Smith got back into office I would return to the Industrial Commission. It was, however, one of the first things he did." But the commission she was appointed to had been completely reorganized during Miller's term in office. It now consisted of a three-member Industrial Board to handle both the judicial work (hearing workmen's compensation cases) and the legislative work (designing codes, or sets of rules, to govern industry) and of a departmental administrator, the Industrial Commissioner. In 1923 Perkins became a member of the Industrial Board, and in 1926 Smith appointed her chairman of the Industrial Board. Smith must have agreed with Perkins's opinion that the Industrial Commissioner was "a total flop," because the governor also asked her to take on many of the commissioner's duties, such as analyzing the budget of the New York State Department of Labor.

Perkins had at least one life-threatening experience while serving on the Industrial Board. A construction worker on an excavation in upstate New York had been hit on the head with a steel bucket, had suffered a concussion, and had received a workmen's compensation award. But after his wounds healed, he began to display symptoms of mental instability. He could no longer keep a job. A claim was made on his behalf that his problem was a result of the injury, but the insurance company refused the claim, making a case that he was a "constitutional mental inferior." Perkins supported the claim that his current problem resulted from the injury he had sustained on the job and brought in medical evidence to that effect. As a result, the man was awarded further compensation, but the insurance company again contested the outcome, and the man still received no money.

Believing that since Perkins had awarded him the money she should pay it to him, the man had come to her office, asked for her, and pulled out a knife. Luckily, she was in the ladies' room at the time, so the deranged man went out into the hall. There, purely by chance, he came upon the man representing the insurance company, whose throat he promptly (but not fatally) cut. Emerging from the washroom, Perkins saw the bloody scene and grabbed the assailant. Help eventually came, the insurance company representative recovered, and the man was institutionalized. But the award for his condition was paid, which helped his family adjust to the new circumstances.

Despite this brush with danger, Perkins loved her job as chairman of the Industrial Board. In fact, in *The Roosevelt I Knew* she described it as "the perfect job." Not only did she feel the job used all her talents, but she also felt it enabled her to make "constant progress toward practical achievement of social justice."

She later recalled some of the achievements she made during this period. For the first time in the history of the New York State Department of Labor, she began to coordinate the work of the Factory Inspection Division and the Workmen's Compensation Division. Until then, a laborer might make a compensation claim because of an accident on the job, but there was no mechanism for informing the factory inspector that a workplace condition needed correction. "So we made a rule that they must report every accident that came in as a compensation claim to the factory inspection division" so that the dangerous condition could be investigated and corrected.

Perkins also took pride in turning the tragedy of factory accidents into an opportunity for new scientific discoveries. For example, no one understood why a bad dust explosion had occurred in an aluminum factory near Massena in northern New York State. Aluminum, after all, is nonflammable. In order to make a nationwide study of the problem, Perkins put together a committee of the National Safety Council, the National Fire Protection Association, and

New York State Department of Labor factory inspectors, laboratory scientists, and industrial hygienists (professionals concerned with the health of industrial workers). The investigators discovered that other unexplained explosions had occurred around the country. As a result of the study, Perkins noted, "We discovered what we now know to be a very real hazard—the dust itself explodes.... Air, itself, is explosive if you get dust into it. It's the electric tensions that are developed between particles when mixed with air that causes the explosion."

Having learned the cause of the problem, Perkins then set about immediately working on a code to regulate conditions in industries that create a lot of dust. She believed that once one became aware of a risk to workers in a particular industry, one had a moral responsibility to regulate it immediately. "If you had knowledge there was a hazard and did nothing about it, then if something happened you were to blame.... So during that period I really pushed very hard for the adoption of many codes."

Another area in which Perkins made progress was in dealing with occupational diseases. At the time, a variety of new chemicals were being put to use in industrial processes before manufacturers were aware of whether or not the chemicals might have toxic side effects. By making them responsible under the law for employee health problems caused by materials in the workplace, Perkins hoped that manufacturers would learn quickly "that it costs money to poison people."

Silicosis, a disease of the lungs caused by inhaling tiny particles of rock and sand, is an occupational disease that Perkins worked hard to control not only as an official of the New York State Department of Labor but also later as secretary of labor of the United States. She ran a statewide contest, offering an award of several hundred dollars to the person who could devise the best method of preventing exposure to silica dust. After awarding the prize, she

arranged for the new device to be installed on a jackham-
mer on the site of the excavation of the foundation for
what was to become New York's Rockefeller Center. The
men working on the site were tested for silicosis before they
began work and after they completed it, and those whose
lungs were clear beforehand also tested clear at the end of
the project. This demonstration that workers could be protected from exposure to silica dust led to the passage of laws
that they must be.

Perkins's achievements as chairman of the Industrial
Board attracted attention in the press both at home and
abroad. *The New York Telegram* of February 2, 1926, for
example, quoted Perkins's description of the new laundry
code the board had just compiled: "It provides for proper
drainage of floors, so workers do not stand in water. It tells
how a machine must be covered so fingers or hands are not
mangled" and called her "one of the worthiest" of those
chosen to serve. And an admiring reporter for England's
Manchester Guardian reported on March 12, 1927, that "I
have met a considerable number and wide range of interesting women in the United States, but none who has
impressed me more than this squarely-built woman....
Under her guidance a comprehensive and enlightened factory code is being worked out and applied, which is trans-
forming factory and workshop conditions as they affect the
safety, health, and comfort of the worker; and worked out
largely in friendly cooperation with employers with the use
of the most up-to-date scientific counsel and advice from
engineering and other experts."

Perkins loved serving under Al Smith and thought him
a wonderful governor, responsive to the needs of the people
of his state. When he was selected to run as the 1928
Democratic candidate for the Presidency of the United
States, Perkins was one of his most active supporters. As she
went around the country speaking on Smith's behalf, she
later recalled, she made it her business to show how Al

Smith's record revealed his "concern and responsibility for the improvement of the social and economic life of the State of New York" and to confirm his promise, as a candidate, "that he would do the same kind of thing at the federal level, although not in identical terms."

But Al Smith was a Roman Catholic, and as he told Perkins in late 1928 after losing the election to Republican Herbert Hoover, "the time just hasn't come when a man can say his beads [pray with a rosary] in the White House." During the campaign, she witnessed some strongly anti-Catholic sentiment the likes of which she had never encountered before. In Independence, Missouri, for example, she was pelted with tomatoes and eggs as she sang Smith's praises before a violent crowd with deaf ears.

Smith had handpicked Franklin D. Roosevelt as the man to run for the New York State governorship on the Democratic ticket. Although it was not easy to convince Roosevelt that he was well enough to take on the task, once he agreed to do so he ran a vigorous campaign. But on election night, as the disappointing national results came in, Roosevelt was certain that if Smith had lost, so had he. That did not turn out to be the case, and once he won office he was determined to be his own man, eager though Smith was to give him guidance. Roosevelt made it clear to Smith that he was going to appoint his own people and make his own decisions.

Because of her husband's continued illness and her mother's death, Perkins was not able to attend the 1928 Democratic convention in Houston, where Al Smith (at podium) was nominated for President. Instead, she listened to his acceptance speech as it was broadcast over the radio.

One of the women who had worked hard for the Democrats in 1928 was Mary Dewson, a colleague of Perkins's from the Consumers'

League and other organizations. Eleanor Roosevelt, the wife of the newly elected governor, was also a mutual colleague of Perkins and Dewson from these organizations. Encouraged by Mrs. Roosevelt, Dewson went to see the governor-elect to ask him to consider two requests: that he advocate a minimum wage law for the state and that he appoint Frances Perkins as his Industrial Commissioner. Roosevelt was agreeable to both requests.

Perkins later learned from Smith that as outgoing governor he had advised his successor to reappoint her to the Industrial Board. Smith had explained to the governor-elect that Perkins had in effect been acting not only as the board's chairman but had also been covering up the inadequacy of the Industrial Commissioner by doing the administrative work for the state Department of Labor. When Roosevelt told Smith he hoped to make Perkins the official Industrial Commissioner, Smith tried to dissuade him, on the grounds that men bridle at taking orders from a woman. But Roosevelt dismissed the advice.

In her biography of Roosevelt, Perkins recounted at length the occasion on which he invited her to serve as Industrial Commissioner in his administration. She recalled being invited out to the Roosevelt home in Hyde Park, New York, where he drove her around in a special car fitted with hand controls. During the drive Roosevelt laughingly told her that Smith had thought the appointment a bad idea and boasted that he was more liberal in his views about women and their abilities than his predecessor. Although Perkins shared the laugh, she loyally spoke up on behalf of her former employer: "But it was more of a victory for Al to bring himself to appoint a woman, never appointed before, when I was unknown, than it is for you when I have a record as a responsible public officer for almost ten years."

In the course of their drive around the property Perkins made sure that if she accepted the new position, Roosevelt would have a clear understanding of just what changes she would hope to make in the Department of Labor and just what legislation she would fight to secure. With regard to changes, she made it clear to him that she believed it was necessary to investigate the administration of the labor department, since she was confident there was considerable corruption. She wanted his commitment that if the investigation turned up any wrongdoing she could fire people, no matter what their political ties. He gave her his word. She also told him that a law passed during a Republican administration had set up an advisory board in the department, but that the board hardly existed except in name. It met only rarely, had no agenda, and had offered essentially no advice to the Industrial Board and the Industrial Commissioner. She wanted his approval to reorganize the advisory board, give it a program, have it meet regularly, and solicit members' advice on actual issues the department was grappling with. He expressed enthusiasm for the idea.

Roosevelt also told her to pursue her entire legislative program, including the passage of laws controlling child labor, further reducing the number of hours of women workers, and prohibiting night work by women. He told her, "I want all these things done. Make all your plans—go as far as you can. When you need help, come to me and I will do everything I can. I am for the program—all of it."

Despite her sense that she would have the governor's support if she accepted his offer, for at least two reasons Perkins was less than anxious to become Industrial Commissioner. On a purely personal level, she was afraid that the job would require her to move to Albany, which would either force her to relocate her daughter, Susanna, now almost 12 years old, or require long periods of separation from her. It might also upset her husband, who continued to go to his office at the Equitable Life Assurance Company (although Perkins was uncertain whether he actu-

KEEP GOOD GOVERNMENT

On election night, 1928, New York gubernatorial candidate Franklin Roosevelt (third from left) and his running mate Colonel Herbert Lehman (second from left) await election results at their campaign headquarters in New York City's Biltmore Hotel. Roosevelt won the election.

ally did any productive work there). On a professional level, there was nothing about the administrative tasks of the Industrial Commissioner that attracted her. She thought she truly preferred her current position, so "despite the pull of a sense of obligation and adventure to take the new one," she told Roosevelt that if something turned up before Inauguration Day to make him change his mind, it would be all right with her, "because I am quite happy doing what I am doing now."

Roosevelt reacted to her offer with surprise and insisted that he had no intention of changing his mind. She later learned that he told a number of people about the escape clause she had offered him. Her behavior seemed to reassure Roosevelt that in Perkins he had found an appointee who would never push her own advantage.

As it turned out, the new administrative position brought with it a substantial raise in salary, to $12,000 a year. It also did not require a move to Albany, because much of the work still centered on the labor department office in New York City. So on January 15, 1929, Frances Perkins (now a few months shy of 49) took the oath of office and assumed the responsibilities of the Industrial Commissioner of New York State.

IN THE MIDST OF A WORLDWIDE ECONOMIC CRISIS

In an article called "Is America a Paradise for Women?" that appeared in *Pictorial Review* in June 1929, novelist Sinclair Lewis argued that it was, while his wife and coauthor Dorothy Thompson took the opposing point of view. As an example of the unlimited professional opportunities he claimed that women had in the United States, Lewis pointed to his former girlfriend: "Miss Frances Perkins, recently appointed State Commissioner of Labor in New York...a position considerably weightier than that of the King of Norway or Sweden or the President of the Irish Free State."

Perkins had been much more humble about her achievement in a speech she gave at a luncheon in honor of the appointment, held at New York's Hotel Astor in February 1929. Putting aside her prepared address, she spoke from her heart: "I take it that we are gathered not so much to celebrate Frances Perkins, the person, as we are to celebrate Frances Perkins as the symbol of an idea. It is an idea that has been at work among us for many years—the idea that social justice is possible in a great industrial community." She thanked a number of people for helping her

After being sworn in as the Industrial Commissioner of the New York State Department of Labor on January 14, 1929, Perkins posed for newspapers photographers along with her daughter Susanna, who had recently celebrated her twelfth birthday.

"since I started on my modest career to improve industrial conditions in this state," including her husband, her daughter, and the women who had helped her raise her child and manage her home.

During most of her first year as Industrial Commissioner, Perkins continued to advance initiatives begun under Governor Al Smith. For example, in order to make sure that every employer in New York State complied with the law to carry workmen's compensation insurance, she first held a publicity drive so that no one could claim ignorance. Then, after warning every employer individually, if employers were still found to lack workmen's compensation policies, "we just [hauled] them in, arrested them and brought them to court."

In her speech at the Hotel Astor, Perkins had spoken of her good fortune in becoming Industrial Commissioner at a time when "industry in general is prosperous." But she was also aware at the time, as she said in *The Roosevelt I Knew,* that "there was a great irregularity in employment." Although the rest of the world still viewed America as a land of bounty, there had been troubling signs in some sectors of the American economy during the previous decade. Farmers, in particular, had not fared well during the 1920s. Many had in fact done so poorly that they could not pay the mortgages on their farms. Because farmers often could not pay their bank loans, many banks in agricultural areas failed. Even though American businesses experienced great prosperity in the period from July 1, 1928, to June 30, 1929, about 550 banks were forced to close their doors during that period.

Textile workers also failed to share in the prosperity of the 1920s. Since New York State was a center of the textile industry and also an important farming state, the problem was a local one. Even though the stock market was still booming, many New Yorkers were experiencing periods of unemployment. Perkins decided that one way to deal with the problem was to revitalize the New York State Public Employment Service. Not only were the offices of the service dirty and chaotic, but the office managers also often had a hostile attitude toward the people they were supposed to serve. Her personal inspection of one office, for example, revealed that applicants for positions were forced to wait in unlit rooms with no seating. The manager claimed that lighting the room would only encourage applicants to steal the bulbs, and providing benches would only encourage them to use the waiting room as a dormitory. With Governor Franklin D. Roosevelt's assistance, she developed an efficient and welcoming State Public Employment Service. The following year, when unemployment intensified, the service was successful in placing tens of thousands of applicants in jobs.

On October 24, 1929, a day remembered as Black Thursday, the stock market crashed. Industrial production had already peaked in August when what is known as the Great Depression began. The Great Depression was an intense business slump that crippled the nation during the 1930s. On Tuesday, October 29, stockholders reacted in panic to the drop in stock prices. Selling their shares at prices far below those at which they had bought them, thousands of people lost fortunes. Not only individuals but also banks and businesses were heavily invested in stocks. Some institutions lost so much money that they were forced to close. Banks had also made loans to individuals and businesses who now could not repay them. As unemployment continued to worsen, many people were forced to withdraw their deposits, and banks sometimes were unable to meet the withdrawal demands. Unlike earlier depressions in the United States, where business began to pick up after a year or two, the economy continued to worsen in this one. Poverty swept through the entire country on a scale previously unimaginable. And the Great Depression also struck elsewhere in the world. In some countries, including

Germany and Japan, dictators came to power who promised to revive the economy but did so by conquering and exploiting neighboring nations.

Perkins, the chief administrator of the New York State Department of Labor, saw signs of the Depression around her on the streets of New York. In a speech on October 23, 1962, she recalled that "people were so alarmed that all through the rest of 1929, 1930, and 1931, the specter of unemployment—of starvation, of hunger, of the wandering boys, of the broken homes, of the families separated while somebody went out to look for work—stalked everywhere. The unpaid rent, the eviction notices, the furniture and bedding on the sidewalk, the old lady weeping over it, the children crying, the father out looking for a truck to move their belongings himself to his sister's flat or some relative's already overcrowded tenement, or just sitting there bewilderedly waiting for some charity officer to come and move him somewhere. I saw goods stay on the sidewalk in front of the same house with the same children weeping on top of the blankets for three days before anybody came to relieve the situation!" She also remembered the unemployed selling apples for a nickel apiece. In her *Reminiscences* she remembered how during her final year as Industrial Commissioner she always carried a large bag of quarters with her as she was driven to work in the mornings in an official state car. At every red light, beggars would open the door of the car and put in their hands. "That seemed to be what was required—a quarter—to anybody who put his hand in."

But she was an optimist and an activist by nature, and she refused to despair. She later recalled asking herself, "Could anything be done or did we have to just accept this blank despair? It would be like saying in the medical field that you had to accept diphtheria as a scourge that exists.... The human race just doesn't lie down under these things." She also disapproved of the policy of President Herbert

According to Perkins, apple sellers began to appear on city streets in 1929: "Some kind-hearted man who had a surplus of apples—because the farmers were in this depression, too— thought of getting rid of his apples (which he couldn't sell) by giving them to the unem- ployed to sell."

Hoover, none of whose efforts to revive the economy had succeeded.

On the way to work one morning in late January 1930, Perkins was aghast to see a front-page story in *The New York Times* reporting Hoover's announcement that there had been a rise in employment in the past week and that the economy was on the upswing. She had been aware of "a bunch of swindlers in the U.S. Department of Labor and Employment Service that were putting out false figures all the time." But she was horrified at the thought that the President, whom she knew to be both educated and intelli- gent, had not bothered to check the figures he had been given.

Rereading the story, she became even more outraged. She could only imagine the effect of this misleading story on the unemployed and their families, who might feel that if their President claimed unemployment was decreasing, their joblessness must result from personal failure.

In her speech almost exactly a year earlier at the Astor Hotel, Perkins had publicly promised, among other things, to "be candid about what I know, of the Labor Department or of the state of industry in this state and in this country. I promise to all of you who have a right to know, the whole truth and nothing but the truth, so far as I can speak it." Without taking into account the respect with which she might have been expected to treat a presidential pronouncement, she called together her state experts and asked them to use the New York unemployment statistics to project a national figure.

The following day, as she recounted in *The Roosevelt I Knew,* she held a press conference in which she issued a statement showing Hoover to be wrong. The unemployment problem was, in fact, worsening, not improving. Satisfied that she had made the truth known, she was taken aback to find herself in the headlines the following day. Both congratulatory and accusatory telegrams and telephone calls streamed in, including a call from Governor Roosevelt. All of a sudden it occurred to her that perhaps she should have checked with him before speaking out against the President. Prepared to apologize to Roosevelt for taking such bold action without his approval, she was surprised "to be greeted by a cheerful voice saying, 'Bully for you! That was a fine statement and I am glad you made it.'" He told her it was just as well she *hadn't* checked with him in advance. "If you had asked me, I would probably have told you not to do it, and I think it is much more wholesome to have it right out in the open."

For the remainder of Hoover's Presidency, whenever the administration issued an unemployment statement, newspaper editors, state officials, and labor leaders asked Perkins to compare the figures against New York State's. She was asked to testify before the Commerce Committee on the unemployment relief bill proposed by her old colleague, now United States Senator Robert F. Wagner. Perkins became the country's highest-profile state labor official.

Later in 1930, Roosevelt agreed with Perkins to appoint a committee to study the current unemployment problem. On March 30, Roosevelt announced the appointment of the Committee on Stabilization of Industry for the Prevention of Unemployment. The committee held public hearings both to educate the people of the state about unemployment and also to collect their ideas.

At Perkins's suggestion the committee was headed by her old friend Henry Bruère, who had done a study of New York City's unemployment while working for Mayor John Purroy Mitchel. Perkins knew that Bruère had not only done a lot of reading on the subject but had also reached some conclusions about what might be done. As she described in *The Roosevelt I Knew,* they were aware that the current problem was much more complicated than the one he had dealt with earlier. "We were in the midst of a world-wide economic crisis." On the other hand, more data on unemployment were now available.

Among the recommendations Bruère had made in his earlier report was that a period of unemployment was the time for a city to undertake major construction. If sewers needed repair, highways needed resurfacing, or schools needed to be built, industry could be revitalized and jobs provided by undertaking these and similar projects. Such public works projects still seemed sensible to Perkins.

Another method that the committee recommended for dealing with the crisis was to spread the available work out among all their employees, having them work shorter hours and fewer days rather than fire anyone. At the time, a six-day week of approximately 10-hour days was the standard working period. Perkins later observed that "nobody had heard of a five-day week until this time. The five-day week was recommended in the State of New York at that time as a method of spreading the work."

The committee submitted its final report on November 13, 1930, shortly after Roosevelt had been reelected to a second term as governor. In addition to a number of specific recommendations, the report expressed this assumption: "The public conscience is not comfortable when good men anxious to work are unable to find employment to support themselves and their families."

Many members of the Committee on Stabilization of Industry agreed that a complicated industrial system should provide a means of unemployment insurance. No state had ever taken such a step before. Since it seemed likely that the cost of such a system would be too much for a single state to carry alone, the committee thought it might be wise to explore a joint system supported by several neighboring states. Perkins suggested to Roosevelt that he call an interstate conference on unemployment.

Perkins, flanked here by two New York State employers, not only initiated but also organized the conference on unemployment that helped Franklin Roosevelt advance toward the Presidency.

Thus, in late January 1931 Roosevelt hosted in Albany

a three-day conference attended by the governors of Massachusetts, Rhode Island, Connecticut, New Jersey, Pennsylvania, Ohio, Maine, and New Hampshire. The conference was one of the high points of his gubernatorial career, revealing his ability to master complex subjects, present them clearly to his counterparts, and guide their thinking. In addition it also fostered relationships that helped Roosevelt later win the Presidency. He enlisted the other governors' support for the idea that unemployment insurance might be desirable and that it might be set up through interstate compacts.

It became clear that Roosevelt had what it took to be a national leader. In December 1931, Roosevelt's supporters sent Mary Dewson, by then head of the New York State Women's Democratic Committee, on an exploratory tour. Canvassing the country to see how a bid by Roosevelt for the Presidency in 1932 might fare, Dewson returned with a favorable report. On March 4, 1932—a year before the next Presidential inauguration would be held—Perkins sent Roosevelt a wire: "This day next year will be interesting." He responded: "I approve your faith."

Perkins later recalled, "I wasn't primarily interested in making Roosevelt President. I was interested in promoting proper labor and social legislation in the State of New York, and if he wanted to be President, in the U.S.A. If Roosevelt was going to be President, or if Smith was going to be President—they were the only two people whose Presidential aspirations I had ever been interested in—my concern was to see that they were Presidents who promoted the line of social justice I thought important."

Whatever her reasons for supporting Roosevelt, support him she did. On the first day of July 1932, the Democratic party nominated Roosevelt for President of the United States. In his acceptance speech the following day he introduced the phrase that would become the byword of his administration. Standing before the convention delegates, he announced, "I pledge you, I pledge myself to a new deal for the American people." Interpreting the phrase's meaning in *The Roosevelt I Knew,* Perkins explained: "the 'new deal' meant that the forgotten man, the little man, the man nobody knew much about, was going to be dealt better cards to play with." (In the years to come Perkins herself would become so closely identified with the New Deal that in the 1977 musical "Annie" she and a colleague, Harold L. Ickes, join Roosevelt in singing "We'll Have a New Deal for Christmas Next Year.")

Her excitement at the prospect of Roosevelt's winning

Roosevelt was cheered by spectators who lined the route he took through Rochester, New York. This appearance came at the beginning of the campaign that would win him the Presidency in 1932.

the Presidency was tempered, however, by the worsening of her husband's condition. Wilson was admitted into a sanitarium in White Plains, New York, sometime in 1932 and remained there until 1937. Sometimes he was in good enough shape to receive friends, play tennis and bridge, and come home for weekends; at other times he was in such bad shape that no one but Perkins could see him.

On November 8, 1932, Roosevelt won a landslide victory for the Presidency. His promise "to restore this country to prosperity" resulted in his carrying all but six states. The country—with bank failures continuing to mount, unemployment soaring, and the lines of the hungry at soup kitchens growing ever longer—was desperate to try a new approach.

Following the election, the newspapers started to speculate about whom Roosevelt might select for his Cabinet. Perkins herself intended to remain as Industrial Commissioner of New York State for the newly elected Democratic governor, Herbert H. Lehman. On December 31, 1932, literally the eve of his departure from the governor's mansion, Roosevelt wrote Perkins a note thanking her for her Christmas letter, expressing his hope of accomplishing "something worth while for the man at the foot of the ladder," and expressing his gratitude for "the fine work you have done these four years."

Earlier that month Perkins had been invited by Grace Abbott, head of the U.S. Department of Labor's Children's Bureau, to speak at a conference of state labor officials in Washington on the problems children were experiencing as a result of the unemployment crisis. Four years earlier an attempt to have Hoover appoint Abbott as his secretary of labor had failed, but it had inspired in women's groups the hope that a woman might soon represent them at the Cabinet level. Now Abbott, along with many others, took part in an effort masterminded by Mary Dewson to convince Roosevelt that Perkins was his best choice for secretary of labor. Abbott had also arranged for Perkins to meet senators and congressmen and to be interviewed and photographed. Years later Perkins reported that she was totally unaware at the time but subsequently learned that she had been invited with the express purpose of getting her "into the public eye at the Washington level."

Soon she began to see reports in the press of the likelihood of her being named secretary of labor. Nonetheless, she went on with her plans to continue in her current position. As she recalled twenty years later, "The idea of moving to Washington horrified me.... My husband was ill in a hospital. I was near him in New York so that I could go to see him regularly and provide easily for his occasional expeditions out of the hospital.... I didn't want to give up living with my child."

Just as four years earlier she had been reluctant to give up her job as chairman of the Industrial Board, she was now reluctant to give up the commissionership. "I liked my job better than any job on earth, and I still do. I still look back at being Industrial Commissioner of the State of New York as *the* most wonderful and beautiful job anybody ever had. I can't think of anything I would rather be." She also felt that the New York State Department of Labor was far superior to the federal department, not only "much more alert" but also with "much better facilities."

Even though she felt quite confident that Roosevelt had no intention of selecting her for his Cabinet and that the rumors were just that, she nonetheless decided to send him a letter clearly stating her lack of interest. On February 1, 1933, she wrote: "You are quoted as saying that the newspaper predictions on Cabinet posts are 80% wrong. I write to say that what they've been printing about me is among the 80% incorrect items." She admitted having been flattered by the numerous letters people had been sending recommending her as secretary of labor. Nonetheless, she advised him that he would be wiser to choose a person "straight from the ranks of some group of organized workers" so that it would be clear "that *labor is in the President's councils.*" She promised that he was welcome to whatever advice and suggestions she might have "at any time & ad. lib. without the necessity of appointing me to anything." While it was true, she added, that her "grave personal difficulties" might make the acceptance of a Cabinet appointment hard for her and "might seriously impair my usefulness to you," she stressed that she wrote not with her own well-being in mind but "for the real advantage of your administration and for the permanent improvement of the status of labor in this country."

Soon after writing the letter, Perkins received a visit from Mary Dewson, by then head of the Woman's Division of the Democratic National Committee. Dewson reported that Roosevelt felt beholden to her for all the Woman's Division had done to help him become elected. Calling in her chips, she had asked Roosevelt to select Perkins as secretary of labor. Dewson therefore needed to know if Perkins would really reject the offer if it was made: "I don't want to go and make a fool of myself any further if you're really going to turn me down."

Then Dewson listed some compelling reasons why Perkins was the right person for the job. The nation was in dire need of someone to promote just the type of social and labor legislation that Perkins had brought about in New York. She had a close personal relationship with Roosevelt, who trusted her implicitly. Furthermore, she said, "You owe it to the women. You probably will have this chance and you must step forward and do it. You mustn't say no. Too many people count on what you do. Too much hangs on it."

Of all of Dewson's reasons, Perkins was most swayed by the last. "I had more sense of obligation," she later remembered, "to do it for the sake of other women than I did for almost any other one thing. It might be that the door would close on them and that weaker women wouldn't have the chance."

In true spiritual anguish as to how she would respond if Roosevelt were to offer her the Cabinet appointment, Perkins took her problem to an Episcopal bishop, Charles K. Gilbert. Gilbert was not only an important figure in the church but also member of a committee formed to urge her appointment. Despite his personal bias, he considered her problem for two days before responding. In a letter to Perkins dated February 11, 1933, he encouraged her to accept the challenge should the President-elect make her the offer. Gilbert reasoned with her that the nation's current economic struggle was far more grave than even a war, and surely she would not withhold her unique God-given talents from the nation in wartime. Telling her that he truly believed that "it is God's own call," he assured her that God would help her through the personal difficulties that lay ahead.

On February 15, 1933, President-elect Roosevelt narrowly escaped assassination after completing a speech in Miami. Anton Cermak, the mayor of Chicago, felled by a bullet in his chest, was not so lucky.

After the events of the past two weeks Perkins now felt that if Roosevelt invited her to serve in his Cabinet, she could not turn down the offer. She was not surprised to be summoned to his office at the Roosevelt house on East 65th Street in New York City on February 22. Even having received his assurances during the interview that he would support her initiatives as secretary of labor, however, she did not accept the offer on the spot. She told Roosevelt that before she could give him a definite answer she would have to check with her husband. Roosevelt asked her to let him know as soon as possible.

The following day she went out to the sanitarium in White Plains, where she knew she would find Wilson "in no state of mind... to have an independent analysis of anything." Nonetheless, "The amenities between my husband and me were such that I would never dream of doing a thing that he hadn't been informed of and consulted about in advance." Perkins was relieved to find Wilson "in a good, controlled mood." She reassured him that he could continue to consider their New York apartment his home and that she would continue to visit him regularly.

She called Roosevelt and accepted the offer, but then proceeded to spend the next several days at home, literally sobbing in terror. Twenty years later she could not recall whether she had actually called Roosevelt again to say she had changed her mind. But if she did make that call, she was sure he had said to her, "Don't be a baby. It'll be all right. Anyhow, it's all fixed and it's going to be given out tomorrow."

On February 28, 1933, Roosevelt publicly announced the appointment of Frances Perkins as secretary of labor. William Green, the president of the American Federation of Labor—the league of labor unions founded in 1886—objected to the appointment. "Labor can never be reconciled to the selection," he announced. At a press conference she called the next day, Perkins told the assembled reporters that Green was "a man of great integrity, vision and patriotism." If he and other leaders of organized labor were not able to find the time to come to see her, "I will hasten to see them."

Reporters also dealt with other issues related to Perkins's appointment. An article in *The Boston Evening Transcript* of March 1, 1933, for example, dismissed the idea that it would be illegal for the secretary of labor to sign official documents with her given name. The article also suggested that "Madam Secretary" was the correct way for the first woman in the Cabinet to be addressed by her colleagues and others.

With her daughter Susanna (now 16 and a junior at the Brearley School in New York City) as her travel companion, Perkins left New York City by train for the inauguration festivities in Washington, D.C. (A first cousin, Jack Johnson, and his sons also came down to Washington from Boston for the inaugural events.) With her she had the new black dress that a friend had chosen for her to wear at the inauguration ball. She also had what *The New Yorker* described as "a transparent paperweight with chemicals in it. You shake it and there stands the Virgin Mary in a pink snowstorm." The paperweight was a good-luck token from Mary Brannigan, one of the women who had scrubbed the floors of the old Industrial Board offices on East 28th Street.

Frances Perkins would need a lot more than this protective talisman to make it through the next 12 years as United States secretary of labor.

THE COST OF A FIVE-DOLLAR DRESS

At the time this article appeared in Survey Graphic *in 1933, Perkins was Industrial Commissioner of the New York State Department of Labor. In the article Perkins warned that buying a five-dollar dress, which was inexpensive in 1933, contributed to the profitability of sweatshops and the exploitation of laborers.*

It hangs in the window of one of the little cash-and-carry stores that now line a street where fashionable New Yorkers used to drive out in their carriages to shop at Tiffany's and Constable's. It is a "supper dress" of silk crepe in "the new red," with medieval sleeves and graceful skirt. A cardboard tag on the shoulder reads: "Special $4.95." Bargain basements and little ready-to-wear shops are filled with similar "specials."

But the manufacturer who pays a living wage for a reasonable week's work under decent conditions cannot turn out attractive silk frocks to retail at $5 or less. The real cost is borne by the workers in the sweatshops that are springing up in hard-pressed communities. Under today's desperate need for work and wages, girls and women are found toiling overtime at power machines and worktables, some of them for paychecks that represent a wage of less than 10 cents a day.

The sweatshop employer is offending against industry's standards, as well as against the standards of the community.... As we have come to know him in New York, this sweatshop proprietor is a "little fellow," doing business on a shoestring.... Since he cannot hope to meet union conditions or the requirements of the labor law, he goes to some outlying suburb where garment factories are not a feature of the local picture and where state inspectors are not on the lookout for him. Or perhaps he goes to a nearby state...where he believes labor laws are less stringent or that he will escape attention.

His work force is made up of wives and daughters of local wage earners who have been out of work for months or even years and whose family situation is desperate. The boss sets the wage rates, figures the pay slips, determines the hours of work. His reply to any complaint is, "Quit if you don't like it."

What is the way out for the conscientious consumer who does not want to buy garments, even at a bargain, made by exploited labor? Common sense will tell the purchaser that someone must pay the price of the well-cut silk dress offered at $4.95. The manufacturer is not producing these frocks for pleasure or for charity. If the purchaser does not pay a price that allows for a subsistence wage and reasonable hours and working conditions, then the cost of the "bargain" must be sweated out of the workers.

The red silk bargain dress in the shop window is a danger signal. It is a warning of the return of the sweatshop, a challenge to us all to reinforce the gains we have made in our long and difficult progress toward a civilized industrial order.

In 1935 Perkins added to her collection of hats as she inspected the Golden Gate Bridge in California, then two years from completion.

5

WRITTEN SO AS TO BE CONSTITUTIONAL

Frances Perkins's personal adjustment to Washington was not easy. For one thing, she felt snubbed on her arrival. The outgoing secretary of labor, William N. Doak, did not reach out to her in any way. The only department employees to make an effort to welcome her were women colleagues: Grace Abbott, chief of the Children's Bureau; Abbott's assistant, Katharine Lenroot; and Mary Anderson, head of the Women's Bureau. Finding affordable and appropriate housing was also a problem. She was still paying rent on a New York apartment where on weekends she joined Susanna (who spent the week living at the home of friends with a daughter in her class). She was also paying private school fees for Susanna and fees for Wilson's institutional care.

The solution to the housing problem came in the offer from another woman colleague that they share a small house in the Washington neighborhood called Georgetown. Perkins had known her roommate, Mary Harriman Rumsey, since 1918, when both women became involved in the Maternity Center Association in New York. The daughter of railroad magnate E. H. Harriman and the widow of sculptor Charles Cary Rumsey, Mary Rumsey had come to Washington hoping to find a way to serve the Roosevelt administration. Since she was a woman of means, Rumsey was able to outfit the Georgetown house with furniture and a staff, but Perkins insisted on paying an equal share of the household expenses.

The women did a great deal of entertaining at their home, where their guests included not only national figures (including their mutual friend Eleanor Roosevelt) but also obscure artists, photographers, poets, and singers. Sadly, this very agreeable arrangement ended with Rumsey's death in December 1934, from complications following a riding accident. Perkins lived alone for the rest of her years in Washington, and her social life suffered. Instead of the casual entertaining on a large scale with a staff to do the work that characterized Perkins's first year and a half in Washington, from 1935 on she entertained infrequently and on a very limited scale.

Whatever Perkins thought would be at the top of her professional agenda on arriving at her new office in March 1933, she surely was not expecting cockroaches and crooks. And yet her very first acts as secretary of labor focused on neither policy nor legislation but on cleaning up the department she inherited—in every way. On her first morning at her new position she discovered cockroaches the size of mice in the desks of her predecessor and his receptionist. After a few weeks roach poison finally eliminated these pests.

An equally distasteful, and potentially more dangerous, task stemmed

Perkins's predecessor as secretary of labor, William N. Doak, did nothing to help her adjust to the post after she was sworn in on March 4, 1933.

from Doak's almost exclusive focus on the deportation of aliens, which at that time was the responsibility of the Department of Labor. Doak had employed a special team of investigators, led by the unscrupulous Murray Garsson, that made spectacular raids without warrants on homes where they believed illegal aliens resided and threw them in jail. More often than not, the terrorized individuals turned out to be either citizens or legal aliens. Luckily, the funding that had supported this dubious gang's activities was about to run out. When Perkins described to Roosevelt what she had learned about Garsson's group, he had a good laugh at his prim and proper appointee's luck in running into a band of crooks. But he agreed with her decision to eliminate them from the department by pleading a lack of funds.

A few nights later Perkins came back to the office to finish up some work, expecting to find no one in the building but the night guard. Instead, as the guard took her upstairs in the elevator, she heard people talking on the fourth floor. When she asked the guard who was there, he explained that Garsson and his team had been there for some time. A little concerned for her personal safety, she asked the overweight, elderly guard to hold the elevator while she confronted the unwelcome visitors. He would not be much help if they threatened her, but maybe his presence would keep them from doing so.

Perkins found the group of men rifling through files and making a pile of the papers they removed from them. She calmly inquired what they were doing. Garsson claimed that the notification that their jobs had been eliminated had been so sudden that they had had no time to clear out their personal belongings and correspondence. Acting quickly, she said they would have to go immediately, leaving all the files behind. If they had anything personal in the building, they could return the next day during office hours, when the staff would assist them in removing what belonged to them.

The expression on the faces of a number of Garsson's associates was threatening. Garsson himself seemed to be weighing the alternatives in his mind: how they could deal with Perkins if they refused to leave versus how they could find incriminating documentation to blackmail others within the future if they failed to hold their ground.

To her relief, Garsson put on his coat to leave, and his men followed his lead. She insisted that they remove not a single piece of paper and demanded they give her the key to the file cabinets. The following day she had the locks changed.

In her first press conference, on March 21, 1933, Perkins announced the abolition of Garsson's group. Reporters for the *Saturday Evening Post* and the *New Yorker* commented that in removing his squad, which had arrested aliens without warrants, Perkins was following in the footsteps of her Revolutionary-era ancestor James Otis. In 1761 Otis had denounced before the chief justice of Massachusetts the practice of empowering British officials to search places for smuggled goods without a warrant. "It's in our family tradition," Perkins told reporters. (In 1947, Garsson and his brother Henry, who was also a member of the gang that ferreted out aliens, were convicted of defrauding the federal government for bribing a congressman to use his influence to promote their business interests.)

Now, with the Department of Labor finally under her control, Perkins could attend to the country's many serious problems that had been on the agenda she had reviewed with Roosevelt only a month earlier. Much of Perkins's first six years as secretary of labor focused on finding a way to discover what she called in *The Roosevelt I Knew* "a method by which federal labor legislation could be written so as to be constitutional." The U.S. Constitution does not empower the federal government to make labor laws or to control the operation of industry within the sovereign states. The Constitution gives the federal government power to intervene only in matters concerning interstate commerce, or business transacted among the states. Perkins reminded readers in her biography of Roosevelt that in the early 1930s "there was no federal labor legislation, and attempts at labor and social legislation on a federal basis had been declared unconstitutional by the Supreme Court."

The first attempt at labor and social legislation with which Perkins became involved was a mixed success. When the New Dealers first came to Washington, she recalled in her *Reminiscences,* "we were improvising under a terrible pressure of poverty, distress, despair.... Therefore, whatever was done was done too quickly to think out all the implications." People from all around the country, not all of them government officials, began to put their heads together to think of schemes to revive the country's economy. At an early Cabinet meeting she learned of two rival schemes to stimulate business. Roosevelt asked Perkins to find out as much as she could about the plans of each group and to report back to him.

With the President's blessing she found her way into a meeting of one of the groups. The outstanding personality there was Hugh Johnson, whom Roosevelt would shortly appoint head of the National Recovery Administration, or NRA. The NRA, an essential element of the National Industrial Recovery Act (NIRA) that Roosevelt signed on June 16, 1933, was one of the first significant New Deal programs to attempt to revive the economy. The act authorized the President to institute industrywide codes with the binding effect of law upon the regulation of the industry. The purpose of the codes was to eliminate unfair trade practices, limit or abolish child labor, establish minimum wages and maximum hours, and guarantee the right of labor to bargain collectively—goals dear to Perkins's heart. (The second essential element of the NIRA instituted a public works program, run by Secretary of the Interior Harold Ickes.)

Perkins accepted every opportunity she was given to explain to the country the purposes of the NRA. In a speech in Brooklyn, New York, for example, she later recalled, "I undertook to show one of the great purposes of the NRA. I said that by starting up the wheels of industry and putting more money in the pay envelopes, there would then be money to spend, and the people who got the pay envelopes with this better wage for a better day's work would have money to spend. They would spend it on merchandise."

Companies that agreed to be bound by the NRA codes were allowed to display a Blue Eagle emblem as a symbol of their cooperation with the NRA. It was Johnson who, as administrator of the NRA, chose the Blue Eagle as a symbol of compliance with the NRA codes. In his book *The Blue Eagle from Egg to Earth* Johnson explained, "To make it possible for...public opinion to support those who were cooperating to create employment and purchasing power and to withhold support from those who were not, there had to be a symbol easily recognizable, striking and effective. We designed the Blue Eagle for this purpose."

The Blue Eagle emblem of the National Recovery Administration saves Uncle Sam from falling on the September 1934 cover of Vanity Fair *magazine.*

From Perkins's first encounter with Johnson, he had impressed her as "an erratic person, but with streaks of genius." Her fears about Johnson's suitability to the task of heading a national recovery movement heightened during a social call paid by wealthy industrialist Bernard Baruch to her Georgetown house. During World War I, Baruch had headed the War Industries Board, on which Hugh Johnson had served. Baruch told Perkins to warn Roosevelt that while Johnson was a fine "number three" man, he was not suited to be the "number one" man. But Roosevelt had already committed himself to Johnson and did not feel he could back out of the agreement.

Perkins was also worried about dictatorial tendencies that she detected in Johnson. At the meeting where she first saw him he seemed completely unconcerned about whether the program he was championing would comply with the U.S. Constitution. Later he gave her a copy of a book, which he greatly admired, written by the Italian dictator Benito Mussolini, who would go on to become an ally of Germany and Japan in World War II. Mussolini's book described the fascist corporate state, led by a dictator who had complete power over all aspects of society, including industry and commerce.

Perkins's fears about Johnson's dictatorial tendencies were shared by others. Johnson held a Blue Eagle parade in New York City on September 13, 1933, in which a quarter of a million people marched. In Johnson's book he described it as "one of the greatest parades ever held in the country." But for some people watching the parade it was too reminiscent of mass rallies in fascist Italy and Nazi Germany. Some claimed that Johnson raised his hand in a fascist salute. In his book Johnson dismissed such claims in an unintentionally amusing passage: "*Time* came out saying I had constantly saluted *au Mussolini* and even had a photograph to prove it, *but it wasn't my arm* on that photograph. It wore the taped cuff sleeve of a cutaway coat and a stiff round cuff with an old fashioned cuff button and I never wore either in my whole life. I think it

Hugh Johnson, head of the National Recovery Administration, described New York City's 1933 Blue Eagle parade as "one of the greatest...ever held in the country," but other people were disturbed by its resemblance to the mass rallies being held in fascist Europe.

was the arm of [the mayor of New York City] which had been faked onto my body."

Eventually Roosevelt came to the conclusion that Johnson, successful as he was in many ways in helping change the country's mood from one of despair to one of hope, really was unsuited to administer an undertaking like the NRA. Among other things, he had a drinking problem that aggravated his mood swings. And he had a tendency to equate criticism with personal betrayal. Not without some difficulty Roosevelt finally succeeded in having Johnson resign, effective October 15, 1934.

A little more than six months later, the Supreme Court ruled that the NRA was unconstitutional, because its codes regulated not only interstate commerce but also commerce within individual states. (The public works part of the National Industrial Recovery Act was not ruled unconstitutional, although some other New Deal measures were.) Perkins later explained the grounds on which its supporters had pinned their hopes for the NRA's constitutionality: "It had been thought that the NRA, by making the agreements to control wages, hours and other matters…just agreements, contracts, had solved the problem. It was thought that you could do by contract between Mr. A. and Mr. B…what you couldn't require them to do by a law."

Although the NRA failed to stand the test of constitutionality, Perkins felt it had succeeded in many ways, some of which she described in *The Roosevelt I Knew:* "The NRA became, in fact, one of the most vital causes of the revival of the American spirit, and signalized emergence from the industrial depression…. Organized labor took a new lease on life. And what is perhaps of most importance to the future, business and labor began to participate with public officers in developing a sound, socially just economic and industrial pattern."

Looking back on her reaction to the Supreme Court's negative ruling, Perkins described her optimism that the successes of the NRA could nonetheless be built on: "It happens not to be my temperament and disposition ever to say that all is lost.... I always think that something can be salvaged out of a wreck." As soon as the NRA was rejected, she became determined "to find some way of introducing, or devising, legislation which would pass the test of the courts, and which would have at least a minimum effect with regard to wages and hours in the U.S.... I began all over studying how to do it."

The first aspect of the NRA to be covered by law after the Supreme Court decision was the right of labor to bargain collectively. The National Labor Relations Act, championed by U.S. Senator Robert Wagner, Perkins's associate from her days as an advisor to the New York State Factory Investigating Commission, became law on July 5, 1935. The act set up an independent federal agency, the National Labor Relations Board, to determine by secret ballot elections whether employees wished to have labor unions represent them in collective bargaining and to prevent or correct unfair labor practices by employers or unions.

In her biography of Roosevelt, Perkins described a conference she had with the President before the negative Supreme Court decision. He laughed at her "New England caution" when she told him that even if the court's ruling was negative, she had two bills locked up in her lower left-hand desk drawer that "will do everything you and I think important under NRA," namely, "putting a floor under wages and a ceiling over hours." The first bill was drafted under the guidance of Harvard law professor Felix Frankfurter, who would later become a justice of the Supreme Court. Frankfurter recommended a strategy that Perkins's colleague Grace Abbott had already used successfully. Abbott had been director of the child labor division of the U.S. Children's Bureau from 1917 to 1919. When the Supreme Court ruled in 1918 that the first federal statute limiting child labor was unconstitutional, Abbott managed

Perkins, still a fairly new secretary of labor, held a ceremonial meeting with steel-workers. Even before she took the position in Washington she had been a long-time supporter of legislation to help establish a minimum wage and maximum working hours.

to continue its policy by having a child labor clause written into all war-goods contracts that the federal government made with private industries for the production of war supplies.

In her *Reminiscences* Perkins recalled, "Felix came up with the idea that since the government can regulate its contracts for purchase with regard to the quality and kind and physical specifications, they could also regulate and by contract agree that certain labor specifications, as to wages, hours, general working conditions, and employment of women and children, be met. As part of the contract which you get to build a ship, or produce so many thousands of yards of yard goods, for the government's purchase, you agree not only as to the quality, character and size of the article that you will make, but you also agree as to the working conditions under which they are made."

The Public Contracts Act, which became law in June 1936, required that workers producing goods under government contracts worth at least $10,000 could work no more than an eight-hour day and a 40-hour week. The act also prescribed that the work be done under safe and healthful conditions and authorized the secretary of labor to set minimum wages based on locally prevailing rates. The Supreme Court later ruled that this act was constitutionally sound in that the federal government had unlimited power to fix the conditions upon which it would make purchases.

In Roosevelt's campaign for the Presidency in 1936, Perkins's main concern was that the Democratic party platform emphasize the need for legislation to replace the NRA codes' control of fair labor standards. As a member of the platform committee, she succeeded in her goal. But it took nearly two years, many political battles, and numerous revisions of the legal wording before the Fair Labor Standards Act, also called the Wages and Hours Act, was finally signed in June 1938. The constitutional basis for the law was that it covered only employees engaged in interstate commerce and persons who "produced goods for interstate commerce." Since the number of people thus engaged totaled some 12 million workers, the Fair Labor Standards Act was at the same time the last major social measure of the New Deal and one of its most extensive. The law not only abolished child labor but also established a minimum wage and set a maximum number of hours that a worker could be obliged to work without being paid at overtime rates. The Supreme Court later confirmed its constitutionality.

When Perkins had met with President-elect Roosevelt on February 22, 1933, and described the programs she would pursue as secretary of labor, her wish list included not only federally mandated minimum wages and maximum hours but also unemployment insurance and old-age insurance. In a speech called "The Roots of Social Security," which Perkins delivered at Social Security Administration headquarters in October 1962, she described how the NRA absorbed so much of everyone's attention for most of the first year of the Roosevelt administration that little attention was paid to this other goal. "It was a little difficult to keep the idea alive, but I took it upon myself to mention unemployment insurance at least every second meeting of the Cabinet—just to mention it so that it wouldn't die; so it wouldn't get out of people's minds."

In June 1934 the President finally got around to appointing a Committee on Economic Security, which he asked Perkins to chair. In *The Roosevelt I Knew* she recalled his saying to her: "You care about this thing. You believe in it. Therefore I know you will put your back to it more than anyone else, and you will drive it through. You will see that something comes out, and we must not delay."

In remarks at the 25th anniversary celebration of the signing of the Social Security Act at the Department of Health, Education, and Welfare on August 15, 1960, Perkins recalled, "The Committee on Economic Security had been appointed, but nobody remembered to have the Congress pass an appropriation for us to work." Thus lacking official funding, the committee was forced to borrow personnel from other departments and universities. It also borrowed money from the Federal Emergency Relief Administration to hire unemployed statisticians, stenographers, and clerks.

As the committee continued to work through the remaining days of 1934, they were hopeful of finding a way to write a Social Security bill that would be firmly rooted in constitutional law. Their inability to decide on an appropriate legal tack to take concerned them, because they knew that if they made the wrong decision the program might be doomed.

While they pondered their indecision, Perkins found herself summoned one Wednesday afternoon at 5:45 to a tea party at the home of Mrs. Harlan F. Stone, the wife of a justice of the Supreme Court. As Perkins recalled in her October 1962 address, "In Washington you don't go to parties just because you want to go, you know; you go because you have to go." Her yielding to social obligation on this

Perkins's private life sometimes intruded on her public accomplishments. In August 1935, immediately after watching President Roosevelt sign the Social Security Act, Perkins left for New York City to help locate her husband, who had been reported missing from his sanitarium.

occasion bore fruit. She found herself sitting in the dining room, teacup in hand, next to Mr. Justice Stone. He asked what progress was being made on the Social Security program, and she admitted, "Well, you know, we are having big troubles, Mr. Justice, because we don't know in this draft of the Economic Security Act, which we are working on—we are not quite sure, you know, what will be a wise method of establishing this law. It is a very difficult constitutional problem, you know. We are guided by this, that and the other case."

According to Perkins, Stone glanced around the room to see if anyone was paying attention to their conversation. Then, directing his words to her alone with a hand cupped around his mouth, he said, "The taxing power, my dear, the taxing power. You can do anything under the taxing power."

With great excitement Perkins returned to her staff and, without revealing the source of her new insight, told them that it was now clear that the program should be based on the government's power to tax.

Just before Christmas, with the committee's report due in early January, Perkins called a meeting at her home to thrash out the final wording. The meeting went on until nearly 2:00 A.M. The Social Security Act, which went to the White House for Roosevelt to sign on August 14, 1935, provided old-age benefits, to be financed by a payroll tax on employers and employees. It also set up a state-federal system of unemployment insurance based on payroll taxes. Less than two years later the Supreme Court confirmed in a seven-to-two ruling the full constitutionality of the new Social Security program, based on the government's broad taxing powers.

As she prepared to leave the Department of Labor for the signing ceremony at the White House, Perkins was summoned to the telephone. Her husband's nurse was calling from New York to alert her to the fact that Wilson had

New York City post-men, photographed in November 1936, display samples of the employee social security blanks they are about to deliver throughout town.

disappeared. Tempted to skip the ceremony to rush to New York to look for him, she thought better of it. If she missed the signing ceremony, the press would want to know why. Immediately after the ceremony was over, Perkins went to the train station and boarded the next train for New York. There, assisted by others, she found Wilson and settled him back into the sanitarium.

This unwelcome experience notwithstanding, by June 1938 Perkins could take pleasure in the knowledge that the main goals on the list she had discussed with Roosevelt more than five years earlier had been accomplished. Unfortunately, during this period of her greatest professional success, the seeds were also being sown for what would turn out to be the greatest torment of her career as a public servant.

On Bloody Thursday — July 5, 1934 — the tension between strikers and the police in San Francisco exploded into violence that left two people dead, 73 injured, and Perkins open to a good deal of inaccurate rumor and harsh criticism.

CHAPTER

6

I Didn't Like the Idea of Being Impeached

Not surprisingly, during her career as secretary of labor Frances Perkins played a role in many strikes. One strike in particular, however—the Pacific Coast longshoremen's strike of 1934—was destined to have an impact on her life that extended far beyond the labor action itself.

A longshoreman is a person employed on the wharf of a port in tasks such as loading and unloading vessels. On May 9, 1934, the longshoremen of San Francisco went out on strike when the local shipowners refused to employ only members of the longshoremen's union. Soon other maritime workers—including sailors, pilots, and engineers—joined the longshoremen in their strike. Shipowners, claiming that the strikers' real aim was to strengthen the power of the Communist party, alarmed many citizens, who knew that the party hoped to overthrow capitalism and establish a dictatorship. The shipowners responded to the strikers by replacing them with workers willing to cross the picket lines, but the strikers retaliated against these "scabs" by breaking their bones or knocking out their teeth.

Soon, alarmed because shipping had come to an absolute standstill all down the West Coast, farmers and

Harry Bridges, chairman of the maritime workers' joint strike committee, was rumored to be a communist. Perkins was attacked, both politically and personally, for refusing to deport him to Australia, his childhood home.

businessmen asked city and state governments to intervene. In response, the governors of California, Oregon, and Washington appealed to Secretary of Labor Perkins to end the strike.

In June the maritime workers chose as chairman of their joint strike committee Harry Bridges, who had for over a decade been a longshoreman in San Francisco active in labor issues, and who was known to associate with Communists. The Department of Labor began an investigation into Bridges's background, turning up nothing more damning than that Bridges—who was born in Australia to a well-off Roman Catholic family, had left home for the sea at age 16, and, still a teenager, had come to the United States in 1920—liked to play the mandolin. Bridges, though not a U.S. citizen, was in the country legally. Investigators found no direct evidence pointing to his membership in the Communist party.

In the meantime, determined to open the port of San Francisco, a large group of merchants decided to employ scab truckers to bring into the city the goods that had piled up along the piers. On July 5, a day that became known as Bloody Thursday, police and strikers engaged in fighting that left two dead and 73 wounded by bullets, clubs, gas, or stones. The following day the governor of California called out the National Guard. On Monday, July 9, thousands of workers lined the streets of San Francisco while thousands more marched in a procession to honor the dead strikers. Unions representing all types of workers in San Francisco voted to express their sympathy with the maritime workers by walking out in a general strike. Analyzing this development, some local newspapers reported that the general strike was an attempted Communist revolution.

As the situation worsened, President Franklin D. Roosevelt was on vacation, aboard a ship sailing from Norfolk, Virginia, to Hawaii. At the last Cabinet meeting before his departure he had put Perkins in charge of the strike situation, but Secretary of State Cordell Hull was Acting President in his absence. (The 25th amendment to the Constitution, which provides for the Vice President to discharge the powers and duties of the President in the event of the President's disability, was not ratified until 1967.)

Perkins later recalled being anxiously summoned by Hull to an emergency meeting in Attorney General Homer Cummings's office. When she arrived in the Department of Justice, she found Hull and Cummings bent over a volume in the library, to find out what the experts said about general strikes. Cummings read out to her a definition of the term "general strike," which stressed that its purpose was the overthrow of the government.

She learned, somewhat to her amusement, that the article they were reading that was alarming them so—what Cummings called "the definitive work on this subject"— was by a former New York State Department of Labor official long dead. She tried to calm them down, dismissing the official's frightening discription as "what an old man, writing a book to sell in his dotage, read out of some European theoretical book. That is pure theory and not reality." She also tried to reassure them by arguing that the strikers had no intention of overthrowing the government. Years later she remained convinced that "it was never intended to be more than a demonstration of sympathy. Of that I am sure.... It was partly also to show the people of San Francisco, and the ship owners in particular, that these men had friends, that labor was strong—watch what you do."

Hull, however, insisted that local government had broken down and that as Acting President it was his responsibility to restore order. He told Perkins that they should prepare to send in the federal troops. Although Perkins was unable to convince him that the strike would be over soon without any calamitous outcome, she was able to keep Hull and Cummings from sending in troops immediately by demanding that they send a message to the President by naval communications and wait for his authorization. She made sure to be first to reach the President, however, and in her communiqué she argued forcefully that sending in troops "would be completely disastrous…and that, as a matter of fact, it was not a general strike. There was no purpose. There was no plan. There was no strike fund. There was no deliberate, spontaneous and purposeful action taken. I said that I could assure him that this strike of different trades would be over in a very few days, if we held off. I said that in the meantime conciliators were at work, and so forth and so on."

As Perkins predicted, the strike began to diminish on its own gradually over the next few days. By the middle of July most workers were back at their jobs. The longshoremen and the shipowners agreed to settle their differences through arbitration—by submitting them to negotiation by a mutually acceptable third party. According to the agreement eventually reached in October, shipowners could hire longshoremen who were not union members, but the dispatcher sending the men out to work would be selected by the union.

But by late summer 1934, despite the fact that the crisis was over and a settlement was in the works, stories began to spread on both coasts that Perkins was a Communist. In the middle of August, when the California chapter of the American Legion (a national society of veterans of the U.S. armed forces) held its state convention in San Francisco, it censured Perkins. They argued that her department was in charge of immigration matters and she had not deported longshoreman leader Harry Bridges, clearly a radical alien. For years to come Perkins would have to endure a campaign aimed at proving her disloyalty to the country.

Sometimes the slander would be hurled at her when she was least expecting it. In March 1935, Perkins, settlement house pioneer Jane Addams, and former President Herbert Hoover were awarded honorary degrees by the University of California at Berkeley. After the ceremony a man passing through the receiving line announced sternly on reaching Perkins, "I will *not* shake hands with a Communist!" Clara Beyer, head of the industrial division in the Children's Bureau and a Berkeley alumna, had accompanied Perkins on the trip. Beyer could do nothing to dislodge a classmate's conviction that Perkins had failed to deport Bridges because they were not only both Communists but were also secretly married.

The stories circulated about Perkins ranged from the merely bizarre—like the story that she was married to or otherwise related to Bridges and was protecting him—to the bizarrely anti-Semitic. A man claiming to be a genealogist visited her sister Ethel at her Worcester, Massachusetts, home. He was doing research, he claimed, into Perkins's lineage back to the 17th century and wanted to know if there was a Jew somewhere in the family tree.

In 1935 a publication appeared with "evidence" that Roosevelt's administration was controlled by six Jews, some of them foreign-born and Communists. Each of the six was pictured within one of the triangles that together make up a Star of David. "Information" about Perkins was included from a pamphlet published by the American Vigilante Intelligence Federation of Chicago: "Frances Perkins says she was born in Boston April 10, 1882. There is no record of her birth in the Boston Register for 1882. Her husband's name is given as Paul Wilson. The only record of marriage of Paul Wilson was at Newton, Massachusetts, in 1910, when he married Matilda *Watski.... Secretary Perkins has decreased alien deportation 60 percent.*" The widely distributed sheet convinced many people that there was at least some truth to the claim.

Unfortunately, the source of some of the misinformation was Perkins's own doing. An examination of her papers at the Mount Holyoke College Archives and Special Collections reveals that sometime between 1915, when she gave the correct year of her birth (1880) on a Census of College Women form, and November 13, 1923, when she filled out a Mount Holyoke questionnaire, she began to claim that she was born in 1882. It is unclear why she began to do so and why she persisted in the claim. To this day some reference books still give the incorrect year of birth for her.

The source of some of the misinformation, of course, is ignorance of the city and the year where her marriage to Wilson took place—New York in 1913, rather than a Boston suburb in 1910. Inaccurate though the marriage "record" was, an anonymous person sent out a mass mailing about the Watski-Wilson union by way of proving that Perkins was pretending to be someone she was not.

In April 1936 Perkins finally had an opportunity to defend herself in public. Mrs. Wagner MacMillan of New York wrote Perkins to say that at her club's meetings she had been hearing rumors about the secretary of labor's background. She insisted that she was not prejudiced against Jews but was disturbed at the possibility that Perkins was falsifying her background. Mrs. MacMillan wanted Perkins to know that she was writing because she was an admirer of hers and simply wanted to learn the truth so that she could set straight the women in her club.

Perkins not only responded in detail to Mrs. MacMillan but also sent a copy of her response to the newspapers. On April 5, 1936, both *The New York Times* and *The New York Herald Tribune,* among others, ran articles excerpting Perkins's response. In a dignified disclaimer of Jewish ancestry she wrote, "If I were a Jew I would make no secret of it. On the contrary, I would be proud to acknowledge it." Perkins went on to disparage the rumors that were being circulated about her: "The utter un-Americanism of such a whispering campaign, the appeal to racial prejudice and the attempt at political propaganda by unworthy innuendo must be repugnant to all honorable men and women." She concluded by expressing both her sorrow that Mrs. MacMillan had been "troubled by this un-American type of propaganda" and her appreciation of the opportunity to clarify the matter. Not everyone, of course, read the newspapers that day, and many people continued to believe the rumors.

The campaign to tarnish Perkins's reputation continued, along with an attempt to prove that Harry Bridges was a Communist. Reports began to come to Department of Labor investigators from individuals claiming to know that Bridges was a Communist. The sources of the stories, however, were not necessarily trustworthy. For example, a man who had given perjured testimony in the past now claimed to have driven Bridges to a Communist meeting. "Whether he was ever a Communist or not, I haven't the remotest idea, even to this day," she later said, but Perkins recalled finding Bridges a straightforward person on whose word she could depend. She remembered, "When I

Finds a Whispering Plot

Herald Tribune photo—Acme
Miss Frances Perkins

Miss Perkins Resents 'Plot' Of Whisperers

Says She Is Not a Jew but Would Be Proud to Own It if Report Were True

From the Herald Tribune Bureau

WASHINGTON, April 4.—Retorting to what she said was a "political whispering campaign," Miss Frances Perkins, Secretary of Labor, declared today that she was not a Jew, that her ancestors were Protestant Christians represented in New England before 1680, and that her name never had been Matilda Wutzki.

"There are no Jews in my ancestry," she said. "If I were a Jew I would make no secret of it. On the contrary, I would be proud to acknowledge it."

Miss Perkins struck out at "this un-American type of propaganda" after she had received a number of letters indicating that a rumor intended to be malicious was in circulation concerning her antecedents.

Charles F. Woods, of the Riverside Public Library, in Riverside, Calif.,

When Perkins was directly asked about her background by a socially prominent woman from New York, she took the opportunity to declare in a letter to the public that rumors about her Jewish ancestry and foreign birth were untrue. Both The New York Times *and* The New York Herald Tribune *(shown here) printed excerpts from her letter. While detailing her British background, Perkins strongly denounced the anti-Semitism behind the rumors.*

would call up Bridges and ask him what had happened or what was going on, he would tell me the exact truth.... I could rely on what he said and I could take action and make my plans on the basis of what he told me being truthful."

In February 1938 Bridges wrote Perkins to say that he was aware that the immigration authorities were considering holding a hearing to decide if he should be deported. She assured him that if the department felt that there were grounds to hold a hearing, she would have a statement sent to him detailing the specific charges so that he could arrange for a defense. On March 2, 1938, the Department of Labor did in fact begin proceedings to deport him.

Perkins later recalled telling her colleagues that the case against Bridges must be dealt with cautiously lest they appear to be deporting him simply because of his success as a labor leader. She remembered thinking that they needed ironclad proof that Bridges was really attempting to overthrow the U.S. government by force and violence "before we tangled in the situation and started to deport him."

But on April 6, 1938, a New Orleans Court of Appeals made a ruling that convinced Perkins to delay the proceedings against Bridges. The court ruled that a Polish immigrant who had belonged to the Communist party for three and a half months in 1932, after which he had applied for U.S. citizenship, could not be deported on the grounds of his brief party membership. Such membership, the court ruled, did not confirm that the Polish-born man supported the violent overthrow of the U.S. government. The Supreme Court agreed to review the case, and Perkins thought it wise to postpone not only the Bridges hearing but also another 11 similar deportation cases until after the Supreme Court made its ruling. Years later she justified her decision: "I thought it was right and proper not to deport people when the court decisions in the different circuits were so varied without a clear knowledge of what the Supreme Court would hold on this matter." To do otherwise, she believed, would be inexcusable: "It was an abuse of executive power for an officer of the government to visit upon and seek to punish an individual, putting him to the expense of defending himself, when the public official knew that the very law and action under which he was proceeding might be upset by a high court review in the near future. You didn't go any further with [such] cases. You left them right there until the court had decided."

In May 1938, the House of Representatives approved the formation of a special investigating committee, the Committee on Un-American Activities, with Congressman Martin Dies, Jr., a Democrat from Texas, as its chairman. The committee's main interest was to identify Communist influences both inside and outside the government. On August 30, Dies sent an open letter to the newspapers insisting that "deportation proceedings against Harry Bridges should be commenced without any further delay." Perkins responded that the hearing was merely being postponed until the relevant Supreme Court ruling was made. From her perspective, merely postponing the hearing against Bridges did not mean she was declaring him blameless. If in the period that it took the Supreme Court to make a ruling Bridges did anything to show that he did favor the violent overthrow of the government, the Department of Labor could still arrest and try him. If it found him guilty, it could deport him. But she said, perhaps naively, "It never occurred to me that this case would turn into the dynamite that it did."

In September, Dies told reporters that if Perkins failed to enforce the law under which Bridges was "clearly deportable" she might face impeachment—a charge of serious misconduct in office brought by the House of Representatives against a government official. The following month Dies made two radio broadcasts carried across the nation accusing Perkins and her subordinates of allowing a "breakdown in the enforcement of our deportation

In a cartoon entitled "Warming up Skirmishes for the Battle of 1939," Perkins and her associates Harold Ickes and Harry Hopkins engage in a snowball fight with Congressman Martin Dies, who hides behind Capitol Hill.

laws." On October 22 an editorial entitled "A Nation-wide Demand for the Resignation of Madam Perkins" appeared in the journal *Liberty*. The editorial asserted that the failure of elected officials "to respect their oath of office presents a situation that seriously threatens the future prosperity of this nation." It questioned whether Perkins could be said to uphold "the principles of our constitution when she refuses to take action to deport Harry Bridges, notwithstanding the complaints and charges made against him by innumerable reputable citizens." The following month, Congressman Dies urged Perkins to resign.

The stress of first the rumors and then the Congressional attack began to take its toll on Perkins. Years later she recalled her bemusement about Dies's motives: "He was a Democrat, after all.... He was youngish. He was well educated.... I had never done anything rude to him.... To this day I have never discovered the reason why he did this." She also remembered with gratitude the members of Congress who came to her defense the first time Dies defamed her: the same Tammany Hall politicians who had watched her career unfold from the time she was a young newcomer to New York City. "But that good bunch of Irishmen... stood up for me.... They weren't going to see me attacked now."

Their defense, however, could do nothing to stop the hate mail that continued to fill her mailbox. She found it harder and harder to fulfill her other professional responsibilities. When she went around the country to speak about Social Security or fair labor standards, for example, during the question period that followed her talk someone from the audience was likely to ask if she were a Communist or if her daughter was Harry Bridges's wife.

Not even all her Cabinet colleagues believed she was doing the right thing in handling the Bridges case so cautiously. In a diary entry dated Saturday, January 7, 1939, Secretary of the Interior Harold Ickes described the Cabinet meeting the previous day in which Perkins for the first time had reviewed for her colleagues the facts about Harry Bridges. As Ickes concluded, "There was not a single one in the lot that would justify the arbitrary expulsion of Bridges from this country.... Bridges himself denies that he has ever belonged to any communist organization. There is no record that he has ever advocated the overthrow of the Government by force and violence.... So far a United States Circuit Court of Appeals has held that he is not deportable and this case is on appeal to the Supreme Court. Yet notwithstanding all this, there is great clamor throughout the land for his deportation, and this has reflected adversely upon Miss Perkins and the Administration."

Despite Ickes's sympathy with Perkins's stance, however, he noted that Postmaster General James A. Farley, who was also chairman of the Democratic National Committee, begged to differ. "He burst in with the remark that, whether Bridges was a communist or not, the people of the country believed that he was and believed that he ought to be deported. He declared that failure to deport him was doing great harm to the Democratic party. In effect, he said that whether he was deportable or not, Bridges ought to be sent out of the country for the sake of the Democratic party." Ickes confided to his diary that he was so appalled by Farley's argument that he was about to announce that "the primary function of a government is to protect the weak," when Roosevelt stated clearly that Bridges should not be deported unless there was unassailable legal proof that he was deportable.

On Tuesday, January 24, 1939, a Republican member of the Dies committee, Congressman J. Parnell Thomas of New Jersey, introduced a resolution calling for the impeachment of Perkins and two of her subordinates, Gerard D. Reilly (the solicitor of labor) and James L. Houghteling (the commissioner of the Immigration and Naturalization Service) on the charge of conspiracy to avoid the enforcement of deportation laws against Harry Bridges. In his diary entry the following Sunday, Ickes—who was no great admirer of Perkins, considering her a long-winded, pushy woman—wrote, "This was an outrageous proceeding."

Perkins herself, in her biography of Roosevelt, reacted to the impeachment resolution with characteristic understatement: "I didn't like the idea of being impeached and was considerably disturbed by the episode." She went on to say, "But Roosevelt, with his complete confidence that if you do the thing that seems right to you, you'll come out all right, patted me on the back in a brotherly way and said, 'Don't worry.'"

To see herself through the ordeal, however, Perkins seems to have needed more than brotherly support. She began during this period to attend church each morning "because it was an easier way to adjust myself to the painful realities of life, and to assure myself of the help and support of God." When she confided in her clergyman that she had difficulty praying to God on behalf of her enemies, he advised her to pray for them not by name but by general category, suggesting that she "pray for those persons who make false accusations. Pray for those persons and then next pray for those persons who make false accusations against you.... Pray that the Lord will enlighten them, forgive their sins and lead them into a way of life in which they will have all spiritual wisdom."

Despite this opportunity for personal religious growth, she still suffered from the experience: "It was a terrible win-

Before their February 8, 1939, appearance before the House Judiciary Committee investigating their impeachment, Perkins jokingly compared herself to Joan of Arc and her colleague Gerard Reilly (with glasses) to the priest who accompanied Joan on her way to the stake.

ter. There was hardly a day when I didn't pick up a paper and read that somebody else had denounced me, or some organization had passed a resolution.... It was extremely painful."

On February 8, Perkins appeared as a voluntary witness before the House Judiciary Committee, accompanied by the department solicitor, Gerard D. Reilly, who was also a subject of the impeachment investigation. Years later she recalled asking Reilly as they walked into the hearing room, "Do you remember the priest that walked beside Joan of Arc when she went to the stake?" She meant her remark as a joke, and he took it as one. When the ordeal was over he said to her, "Until you made that joke to me I was fairly trembling inside with dread at this occasion, but when you made a joke, it was all right." Perkins remembered feeling as she entered the room "that this might be a den of lions, but I must not be afraid."

After reading a prepared statement, she asked the members of the House Judiciary Committee if they had questions for her. Reilly later said to her that at that moment "you could see them all sharpening their knives and their pencils." She recalled being grilled by more than half the committee, some of whom revealed their sympathy while others revealed their loathing.

She apparently handled herself well, because on March 24 the Judiciary Committee reported to the full House that "after careful consideration of all the evidence in this case, this Committee is unanimous in its opinion that sufficient facts have not been presented or adduced to warrant the interposition of the constitutional powers of impeachment by the House." Nonetheless, the 10 Republican members of the committee added their "Additional Views." Arguing that Perkins and her subordinates had been "lenient and indulgent to Harry Bridges," they concluded, "This course of conduct which we condemn does not justify impeachment, but it does call for the official and public disapproval of this Committee."

The House tabled the impeachment resolution, but somehow that did not become national news. On April 3, Congressman John A. Martin of Colorado, who had never met Perkins, asked the Speaker of the House for an opportunity to make some official comments on the dismissal of the impeachment hearings against her. He spoke of his regret that "after months of Nation-wide publicizing of unjust and unfounded charges against a public official, the final result is heralded by no blare of trumpets and is scarcely brought to the notice of the public, which for months and months has been fed with promises that a national public official would be shown to have been guilty of high crimes and misdemeanors and of betrayal of public trust...." He went on to express his concern that so little attention was paid to the exoneration of Perkins and her associates, while had they been impeached there would have been extensive press coverage. He argued that simply finding Perkins, Reilly, and Houghteling innocent of the charges was not enough; the rumor campaign must be criticized and stopped: "All fair-minded people should reprobate and condemn the campaign carried on against them, more pregnant with possibilities of danger to our institutions than even the subversive forces they were charged with being in league with."

Two weeks after Congressman Martin's impassioned speech was written into the Congressional Record, the Supreme Court ruled that an alien who joins the Communist party after entering the United States "is not deportable on that ground if at the time of his arrest his membership has ceased." Now, before it could deport Harry Bridges, the Department of Labor's Immigration Bureau would have to prove that he had been a member of the Communist party on March 2, 1938, when the warrant for his arrest was issued.

Perkins selected the dean of Harvard Law School, James Landis, to conduct the hearings against Bridges, held that summer on Angel Island in San Francisco Bay. According to Perkins, that site—a half hour by boat from San Francisco—was chosen because witnesses who claimed to be afraid of being set upon by Bridges's "goons" could be guaranteed protection there. On December 28, 1939, Landis delivered his report to Perkins. He concluded that "the evidence...establishes neither that Harry R. Bridges is a member of nor affiliated with the Communist party of the United States of America." The Bridges case was reopened several times over the following years, with two deportation orders being made and then reversed, the second time by the Supreme Court itself. Bridges became a citizen of the United States in September 1945.

Congressman Martin had concluded his congressional address in April 1939 by saying, "The word 'finis' has been written on this abortive attempt to destroy the first woman ever to have the honor of a seat in the Cabinet." But that assertion was wishful thinking. On May 27, 1940, Congressman John Tabor of New York spoke about the impending vote on Roosevelt's plan to shift the Immigration Bureau from the Department of Labor to the

Department of Justice in terms unflattering both to Perkins and to her boss: "We are going to vote for this reorganization plan because the President has not the patriotism nor the courage to remove the Secretary of Labor, a notorious incompetent, and one who for the last seven years has steadily and steadfastly refused to enforce the Immigration Law."

Many people understood Roosevelt's decision to transfer the Immigration Bureau out of the Department of Labor as a sign of his lack of confidence in Perkins. In fact, as she later recalled, she had been urging him since her first days in office "that the Immigration Service be taken out of the Department of Labor. It ruined the Department of Labor. It overshadowed our proper functions in the time and money that it consumed. I didn't care where it went." Before announcing his decision, Roosevelt had the courtesy to call her at home to inform her. He explained that he was moving the bureau not to the Department of the Interior, which was where she thought it belonged, but rather to the Department of Justice, because of the rising number of spies

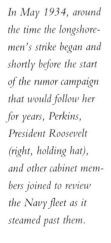

In May 1934, around the time the longshoremen's strike began and shortly before the start of the rumor campaign that would follow her for years, Perkins, President Roosevelt (right, holding hat), and other cabinet members joined to review the Navy fleet as it steamed past them.

and saboteurs who were infiltrating the United States now that World War II had broken out in Europe. Perkins always rejected the argument that shifting the immigration bureau out of her department revealed Roosevelt's displeasure with her in some way: "Well, getting back to the Immigration Service, the President didn't walk over me on that. That was following out my recommendation, somewhat belatedly."

The denigration of Perkins continued in mainstream and fringe publications alike. On July 27, 1940, an article in the *Saturday Evening Post* claimed that "Miss Perkins is not a Communist, not even remotely a Communist sympathizer. She is as true a democrat in her convictions as I have ever known. But she represents the classic type of soft-minded liberal whom the Stalinists behind the scenes know how to exploit for their own purposes." On Sunday, September 15, 1940, Harold Ickes reported in his diary that he had been shown a pamphlet, "The Fifth Column in Washington," the aim of which "is clearly to pin the label of communism on the Administration." Perkins was among those named as "communist sympathizers, or worse."

The attack on Perkins also continued in the House of Representatives. On November 10, 1941, Congressman Phillip A. Bennett of Missouri referred in a speech in the House to "Frances (Wadski) Perkins" and to "her native Russia." He went on to say, "surrounded as she is by Communists...." Although later in the month he corrected what he had said about her place of birth and her name, he did not withdraw his statement about her Communist associations.

Ironically enough, within a few years Frances Perkins would, as Civil Service Commissioner of the United States, be entrusted with evaluating the loyalty of other government employees who were accused of having Communist ties. But before that career move came, she was to live through a second world war.

The warm personal relationship between President Roosevelt and his secretary of labor is apparent in this photograph. It was taken on December 17, 1943, after Roosevelt's return from the Teheran Conference, where he discussed military and political issues with British prime minister Winston Churchill and Soviet premier Joseph Stalin.

ALL THE REWARD I COULD EVER HAVE ASKED

In late 1938 or early 1939, as Germany and Japan became ever more aggressive toward their neighbors, Perkins wrote in her personal files the following question about Roosevelt: "Does he dream of war?" Perkins herself was convinced that a war involving the United States was inevitable. She never forgot where she was and how she reacted when she first learned of the German invasion of Poland on September 1, 1939. Seated on the doorstep of the family house in Maine, about to set off by car for Boston to catch a train to Washington, she heard the news over the car radio. Turning to her family she said, "We'll be in the war. The world war has begun and we will be in it. It's inevitable."

She also recalled an emergency Cabinet meeting being called after the invasion of Poland. She had by now been a Cabinet member for nearly six and a half years, but this meeting was memorable. "I had never heard profanity in that Cabinet until that day.... But on this occasion when their emotions were all so deeply stirred by the breaking out of the war—everyone was upset with the invasion of Poland, the terrible war happening, the broken words and treaties—there was terrific profanity."

Perkins had no doubt in her mind as to the important issues and values at stake in this war. She remembered thinking "that if we, Western civilization, did not come out on top, nothing would have any value…. All Europe was overrun by a tyrannical mob." She never questioned whether this was a war worth fighting: "I was anything but a pacifist."

When the war broke out in Europe, the United States was some months away from the 1940 Presidential election campaign. On July 18 the Democratic party broke a long-standing tradition of limiting the Presidency to two terms by nominating Roosevelt for a third term. Perkins recalled being against the idea of a third term "on principle," but she couldn't think of anyone else who could lead the country through war as well as Roosevelt. The situation in Europe was worsening by the day, with the Nazis occupying Scandinavia in April 1940, the Netherlands and Belgium in May, and Paris in June. German attacks on

According to Secretary of the Interior Harold L. Ickes (who was not present when the photograph was taken), at this special session of the Cabinet on Tuesday, September 27, 1938, "the European situation was the almost exclusive subject for discussion…so that if war started there could be no doubt in the mind of anyone" that Germany, not the United States or any of its allies, "was responsible for starting it."

Britain by air commenced, then intensified. During 1940 the Nazis also ordered the Jews of Poland into walled ghettos as Hitler's plan to rid Europe of its "inferior" groups began to unfold.

According to his wife, Eleanor, Roosevelt himself had been ambivalent about seeking a third term. In her book *This I Remember* she explained that while he had never said so explicitly, she gathered from offhand comments of his—about books and articles he would like to write, about wanting to spend more time in a little stone cottage he had had built at Hyde Park—that he longed for some peace and quiet. But once he was nominated, he felt an obligation to run. "In his mind, I think, there was a great seesaw: on one end, the weariness which had already begun, and the desire to be at home and his own master; on the other end, the overwhelming interest which was the culmination of a lifetime of preparation and work, and the desire to see and to have a hand in the affairs of the world in that crucial period."

Roosevelt's opponent in the race was Republican Wendell Willkie, whom Roosevelt defeated handily on November 5. From Perkins's point of view, one of Willkie's blunders in running his campaign was made during a pro-labor speech he gave in Pittsburgh. Instead of playing it safe by simply promising to appoint a secretary of labor from the ranks of labor, when the applause died down he stuck his foot in his mouth by adding, "And it won't be a woman, either!" Roosevelt and Perkins later agreed that Willkie had thus unnecessarily alienated women voters.

Perkins campaigned vigorously for Roosevelt. She remembered questioning him how to respond if people asked about the possibility of war. "He said, 'The good safe line is to say that the United States will not fight unless attacked. That's always safe.'" She thought she would do better, however, to try to steer clear of the question of war completely.

According to Perkins, shown here at a dinner at the 1940 Democratic national convention in Chicago, the reason to go to gatherings like these was "just to be there, circulate, use influence, and be pleasant to everybody, the way you do at conventions."

Perkins recalled giving a campaign speech on Labor Day 1940 from a radio station in Boston, as was her annual custom. In it she summarized what the Roosevelt administration had done on behalf of labor, "including the recognition of labor as a partner in collective bargaining, treating them fairly, together with all the legislation that was aimed at the improvement of the lot of labor.... We had the Social Security program, the National Labor Relations Act, the Wage-Hour legislation.... It was a good speech."

Although Perkins was glad to endorse a third term for Roosevelt, she felt that two terms as secretary of labor were all that she wished to serve. She had accomplished nearly all the things on the list she had reviewed with Roosevelt in his New York City study in February 1933. The personal attacks on her had taken their toll. In addition, she felt on principle that it was time for some new blood: "I had been there as long as I thought anybody ought to be there.... Politically speaking, it's a good thing to have a turnover." After the election she arranged a meeting with Roosevelt on a Sunday afternoon at the White House. While she tried to explain to him her reasons for resigning, he sat and worked on his stamp collection. But instead of giving her an answer, he talked at her for over an hour and a half about the idea of an international currency based on a unit of energy called the erg.

Perkins did not give up the attempt to resign, however, and from time to time during December she brought up the subject again. He would always tell her he had had no time to consider it. She, however, was eager to get on to the next stage of her life and knew that there were a number of positions that would be open to her if she would only say the word. On the other hand, she had no intention of leaving Roosevelt in the lurch and wanted to help him in any way she could. Years later she recalled telling him in one of their conversations: "If you want me to stay around, I'll do the most stupid chores. I'll take a lower title, a lower grade, anything where I don't show or don't have any responsibility apparently, if it's something I can help you on. You can put me on some darned advisory committee, if you want to. I would really like to be released and I would like to have it done so that I can go get myself a proper place in life now." What exactly she meant by "a proper place" is not clear.

When she saw that badgering him on the subject was getting her nowhere, she enlisted Mrs. Roosevelt on her behalf. A week or so later she received a letter from Mrs. Roosevelt, a brief summary of which was that "I have talked to him about it, and the answer is no, absolutely no." With the situation in Europe worsening, Mrs. Roosevelt added, "He's got to think about the war, the appropriate diplomacy, the foreign problems and all that. He just can't put his mind on a new person operating in this field. You do understand each other. That's that. It can't be done."

After the next Cabinet meeting Roosevelt held her back and asked her if she had heard from "My Mrs." He went on to say, "You know me. You see lots of things that most people don't see. You keep me guarded against a lot of things that no new man walking in here would protect me from."

Perkins finally gave up the quest. She understood that "he had come to have confidence in me. It was a very personal relationship. That was all there was to it." In any case, there was no truly compelling reason for her to leave. "My personal and private situation was no worse than it had been for eight years." Her daughter, now nearly 24, was a married woman. Her husband had left the sanitarium in 1937 and was living in a facility in North Carolina, where he continued to be treated medically as necessary. She understood, too, that as the war clouds thickened, labor and social justice issues would have to take a back seat to the war effort. She knew that with herself at the head of the Department of Labor, Roosevelt could be certain that she would continue to keep those matters "going in what he regarded as a right direction."

On December 29, 1940, Roosevelt gave one of his "fireside chats," radio broadcasts to the American people that were also listened to around the world. In this broadcast he described the United States as being the "arsenal of democracy." He told his listeners that he was determined to keep America out of the war, but promised to increase his country's war aid to those "in the front lines of democracy's battle" who were fighting Nazi Germany.

With the expectations that war would break out sooner or later, that eventually the United States would be drawn into it, and that it would be a long one, Perkins began to prepare her department for these eventualities. She knew that preparing for an unknown situation was not going to be easy: "You have to be able to foresee, to project your mind into a situation that never has been, and to think out how you could collect the information necessary to answer the questions that will certainly be raised. You first have to think

QUICK, DELILAH! THE SHEARS!

PERKINS

DEFENSE

CIO

AID TO DEMOCRACY

SAMSON

This 1941 cartoon compares Perkins—in her trademark tricorn hat and pearls—to the biblical figure Delilah, and the Congress of Industrial Organizations (CIO), a labor organization, to a modern-day Samson. The CIO led strikes that threaten to slow down war production, and the government hoped that Perkins would use her "shears" and force the CIO to back down.

out what the questions will be and then think out how you will find the method by which you can answer them."

She began by calling a staff meeting of her top people and instructing them to think about what the department should do in case of war. Aware that the Bureau of Labor Statistics would play a key role in the war, she made sure that the appropriate topics and methods of research were under consideration. She recalled thinking that the bureau's "first service to the rest of the government would be to know what was going to be needed in the way of materials and manpower and operations and expansion, as well as cost of living and all that sort of thing, and what was going to be needed in the way of wages, what wage changes were going to be, what modification in the hours law there would have to be." Thanks to the bureau's statistical analyses, the department was able to provide the draft board "with a call-up principle and pattern" and to advise the country's manufacturers on how much additional hiring would be necessary. "We figured out, for instance, how many man hours of labor it would take to provide for the expansion of, we'll say, a heavy industry operation which was now going to be turned into a war supplies operation."

Perkins also instructed Katharine Lenroot, head of the department's Children's Bureau, to make plans to evacuate and care for children in wartime and also to make a list of special safeguards to protect the youngsters who would certainly be asked to work during the war effort. Under Perkins's direction the Children's Bureau and the Bureau of Labor Standards collaborated "to set up standards well in advance for what we could foresee plainly would be the demand for greater employment of young persons—that is, persons who ordinarily would be expected to remain in school.... We recognized the hazards that there were, both in the matter of exhaustion and fatigue, and also in the matter of dangerous machinery and accidents, to inexperienced young people. So we drew up a set of standards."

Until the middle of June 1940 the Immigration Bureau was also under the jurisdiction of the Department of Labor. Because it was clear that the infiltration of spies would be a problem, Perkins led the bureau in "tightening up the controls... by which we could distinguish a possible entry who might be a spy."

Before helping her own department adapt to the likelihood of America's entering the international conflict, Perkins had earlier played a role in the Civilian Conservation Corps (CCC), a New Deal program that, however inadvertently, also helped the nation prepare for war. The CCC was the Roosevelt administration's first act in the field of relief. An early environmentalist, Roosevelt had the idea of recruiting large numbers of the unemployed to plant trees, build dams and flood barriers, fight forest fires, maintain forest roads and trails, and otherwise help conserve and develop natural resources. At its largest the CCC employed 500,000 men, and over the years it provided work for a total of 3 million people. The Department of

Labor under Perkins was in charge of enrolling men for the program. Although it was abolished by Congress in 1942 after the United States entered World War II, until then the CCC helped prepare its recruits for military discipline by training them to follow orders and live in work camps run by the army.

In the summer of 1941, while the Department of Labor was modifying its work to prepare for a war emergency, Perkins was invited to and attended a luncheon given by the wife of the Japanese ambassador at the embassy. She remembered the tension at the event. "We smiled all the time. It was obvious that this was the first brigade answering the Secretary of State's request for good social relationships between the Japanese embassy and the officials of Washington."

But such attempts at a good relationship were destined to fail. On Sunday, December 7, 1941, the Japanese carried out a surprise attack on the U.S. military base at Hawaii's Pearl Harbor. Within two hours of nonstop attack, some 360 Japanese warplanes sank or seriously damaged eight U.S. battleships, destroyed 200 aircraft, killed more than 2,000 sailors and nearly 400 other people, and wounded another 1,300.

As she was working with a stenographer on a report in New York that weekend, Perkins was interrupted by a phone call from her chauffeur. While attending a game at a ballpark he had heard that a Cabinet meeting had been called for that night, and he wanted to know the arrangements for picking her up. Then the White House telephone operator called to inform her of an 8:00 P.M. Cabinet meeting. She still did not know the reason for the emergency meeting.

Secretary of the Interior Harold Ickes was lying down at his home when the call summoning him to the meeting came. In a diary entry written exactly a week later he recalled the throngs of "quiet and serious" people standing around the White House as he approached. He also recalled Roosevelt's unusually serious demeanor. "He began by saying that it was probably the most serious situation that had confronted any Cabinet since 1861. Then he started to give us the news that had come in to him, apparently without holding any of it back." The President read his Cabinet members a message he had prepared for delivery the following morning to a joint session of Congress, calling for Congress to declare that a state of war had existed between Japan and the United States from the time of the attack on Pearl Harbor. He told the Cabinet that he anticipated that Germany and Italy would declare war against the United States, in which case he would also ask Congress to declare war against those countries.

Perkins went into her office at the Department of Labor very early the following morning, well before the President's scheduled address to Congress. She felt that just as family members need parental guidance in a time of trouble, her professional family needed its leader's support and guidance now. "All I could say to them was the appropriate thing to say under any conditions of disaster, 'We will find the strength to meet this. We will meet it.'"

Despite the advice of Perkins and other Cabinet members, Roosevelt decided to run the war effort through a series of independent agencies set up specifically for that purpose. Perkins always felt that her department could have done better than the War Labor Board, but she was glad to have her department's Bureau of Labor Statistics serve as its research arm and her department's Conciliation Service (which promoted cooperation between labor unions and employers) make its expertise available to it. Without agreeing with the President's decision to set up these special agencies, she also understood why he did so. He understood the potential danger the government's assumption of war powers presented to a democracy, and newly created agencies could be quickly disbanded after the war.

Although the Department of Labor thus had a much smaller direct role in the World War II war effort than it had had in World War I, Roosevelt still could, at least in fun, imagine Perkins administering a much greater undertaking than her own department. In Eleanor Roosevelt's *This I Remember* she described an event that took place in a 1942 dinner the Roosevelts gave for his Cabinet at the White House. In earlier administrations, each Cabinet member had given a dinner for the President and his wife, but because of Roosevelt's disability, during his administration the Cabinet gave a single dinner once a year at a hotel. During the war, however, the Secret Service advised them that it would be too great a security risk for the President to eat at a hotel, and so the dinner was held at the White House and hosted by the First Couple. The security risk idea seemed to tickle Roosevelt's fancy, according to Mrs. Roosevelt. "Franklin was very much amused, and during dinner said: 'What a wonderful opportunity this would be for Hitler if he could just drop a bomb on the White House and catch so many important people at one gathering. If all of us except Frances were killed, we would have a woman President.' "

When Perkins first came to Washington in 1933, unemployment was one of her major professional concerns. About one in four heads of households—some 13 million people—were out of work. While the New Deal programs she helped push through renewed the confidence of the American people in their government, about 15 percent of the U.S. work force was still out of work in 1940. But the great increase in the production of war materials provided so many employment opportunities that by 1944 the unemployment rate fell to only about 1 percent.

One American who looked for work but did not succeed was Paul Wilson. Among his wife's papers in Columbia University's Rare Book and Manuscript Library is a poignant letter, dated May 12, 1942, which Wilson apparently sent to a number of people. In it he explained that now that his health had improved, he hoped to be able to take the place of some young man who was away at war. He described his employment history at the Bureau of Municipal Research and the Equitable Life Assurance Society, as well as his experience with the U.S. Shipping Board during World War I, and from time to time with legislative investigative commissions seeking expert advice in dealing with municipal, county, and state budgetary matters and taxation. Wilson's plea to make himself useful at a time of national need went unheeded, however, and he remained out of work.

In the summer of 1944, the U.S. Presidential election campaign unfolded against a backdrop of stunning U.S. and British military breakthroughs in Europe. With much of the country unwilling to switch leaders in mid-war, Roosevelt was nominated for an unprecedented fourth term. Running on the ticket with him as Vice President was Senator Harry S. Truman of Missouri. On November 7, the Democratic ticket defeated the Republican nominee, Governor Thomas E. Dewey of New York.

A little more than a month before election day, on October 4, 1944, Perkins had occasion to mourn the death of a former New York governor, Al Smith. Despite the tensions that had separated Roosevelt from his former mentor Smith, Perkins had managed to keep up a relationship with Smith during her years in Washington. In New York to pay her last respects to Smith, she told a reporter, "I do not think it is now generally realized that Al Smith was the man responsible for the first drift in the United States toward the conception that political responsibility involved a duty to improve the life of the people."

An associate of Perkins's, also in New York for the services, overheard a conversation among some old Tammany Hall politicians, who were wondering what had turned Smith into a reformer who had done so much for the people of New York. One of them spoke up: "I'll tell you. Al Smith read a book. That book was a person, and her name was Frances Perkins. She told him all these things and he believed her."

Little did she or any of those mourning Smith that October day suspect that only a little over six months later they would be mourning Smith's successor to the New York State governor's mansion. In *The Roosevelt I Knew* Perkins denied suspecting that Roosevelt's health had begun to fail when he accepted the nomination. She was aware, of course, of the "terrible, unceasing strains of wartime demands and the constant need to make decisions which would be far reaching and have favorable or disastrous consequences." He had obviously aged during his terms of office, but so had she, and he still had a good appetite and was always ready for fun. It was only at the Cabinet meeting on the Friday afternoon before inauguration day that she began to worry about Roosevelt's health. She was concerned to see how thin he had become.

Perkins came to that meeting expecting him to announce her resignation at it. Sometime after the election she had asked him to accept her resignation, and he had seemed to do so. They had discussed possible successors, but he had asked her to make no official announcement until he had decided who would fill her shoes. In the meantime, Perkins had told her closest colleagues at work that she would be leaving. She began to pack up her personal belongings. But on the eve of inauguration day Roosevelt remained silent on the matter.

So after the Cabinet meeting was over, she had a private conversation with him, urging him to make the announcement now. He rejected the thought out of hand. He told her he was too preoccupied right then to contemplate such a change. In a tired voice he spoke to her from his heart, in what she would always consider their parting, even though she saw him again on several other occasions.

Putting his hand over hers, with tears filling his eyes, he thanked her for everything she had accomplished despite all that she had been through. In her biography of Roosevelt she wrote, "It was all the reward that I could ever have asked—to know that he had recognized the storms and trials I had faced in developing our program, to know that he appreciated the program and thought well of it, and that he was grateful."

Perkins realized that this was not the time to push the question of her resignation. It could wait until a time when the pressures of war had lightened.

The following morning she was at the inauguration ceremony. Although in *The Roosevelt I Knew* she described the President as looking much healthier than the previous afternoon, Harry Truman decades later recalled her emotion at the sight of the thin Roosevelt, clearly in pain, delivering a very short inaugural address. "He stood there in the cold…and his hands shook, and his voice was not steady. I remember Frances Perkins was crying, I think. But she was careful not to let Roosevelt see her."

On January 22, 1945, two days after the inauguration, Roosevelt sent Perkins a letter, repeating that her resignation "is hereby declined. Indeed, it is rejected and refused."

In late March, Perkins had her last meeting with Roosevelt. In a conversation of 15 or 20 minutes she reviewed a small agenda with him. He told her in confidence that he believed the war in Europe would be over by May. The next day he left for Warm Springs, Georgia, a spa to which he retreated periodically for water therapy to treat the symptoms of his polio.

In the late afternoon of April 12, 1945, less than a month before V-E Day—the day of victory in Europe for the United States and its allies—Franklin Roosevelt died of a cerebral hemorrhage at Warm Springs. Earlier in the day he had posed for a portrait. Later, sitting at a card table signing papers, he had complained of a terrible headache.

Perkins was sitting at her desk conferring with an official from the State Department about a forthcoming International Labor Organization conference when a call came from the White House. There would be a 6:00 P.M. Cabinet meeting that night. She later recalled saying to her colleague, "Either the War is over and there's an offer to surrender—or, the President is dead."

Perkins was the first Cabinet member to arrive at the meeting room. There Harry Truman himself confirmed her second guess. At 7:09 P.M. Truman took the oath of office and assumed the Presidency. For a change Perkins was not the only woman in the room—Truman's wife and daughter witnessed the historic event too.

Later that week she attended both the funeral held in the East Room of the White House and the burial ceremony at a plot near the Roosevelt home in Hyde Park, New York. Several years earlier, Roosevelt had pointed out to her the spot in the rose garden that he had chosen as his grave site.

According to an appointment sheet dated May 21, 1945, among Harry Truman's private papers, Perkins came to see the new President at 11:15 that day to discuss her resignation. "She told me ever since 1936 she had been trying to leave the Department but that President Roosevelt could not get along without her—she now felt I should have a Cabinet of my own choosing and she would like very much to quit. I reluctantly accepted her resignation."

Just how reluctant Truman was to see Perkins go is not clear. In an unsent letter to one of his biographers, dated February 26, 1950, Truman described the backgrounds and abilities of the individual members of the Cabinet he inherited on April 12, 1945. In that note he called Perkins "a grand lady—but no politician. F.D.R. had removed every bureau and power she had." In his *Memoirs* Truman also expressed the fact that he "held her in very high regard and believed she had done a good job despite the fact that many of her responsibilities had been taken from the department by the emergency agencies," as well as his belief that the labor department "had been virtually dormant."

Truman chose as her successor Lewis B. Schwellenbach, a former U.S. senator and federal judge from Washington State, who would officially take over the Department of Labor on July 1, 1945. Perkins tried to be more helpful to Schwellenbach than William N. Doak had been to her 12 years earlier, but Schwellenbach rebuffed her every overture. She later recalled, "He wasn't even polite to me."

Nor was Schwellenbach polite to her staff. On July 2 he issued an insulting order to the entire department, which the Washington *Evening Star* published on its front page: "It is the function of this Department to execute the laws. The duty of an officer in this Department is to accept the laws as Congress has written them and as the Courts have interpreted them. The fact that he may think the Congress should have written, or the Courts should have interpreted, the law differently in no case justifies him in ignoring or attempting to circumvent the law. I will expect full cooperation on this policy."

On June 27, a few nights before her tenure in office ended, a testimonial dinner was held in Perkins's honor at the Mayflower Hotel in Washington, D.C. Among the speakers singing her praises was William Green, the president of the American Federation of Labor, who had taken such strong objection to her appointment 12 years earlier. So gracious were his remarks that in her own speech Perkins made the audience laugh by noting how pleased she was that on the eve of her retirement organized labor had finally come to appreciate her.

Another eloquent tribute that night came from Senator Robert F. Wagner, Perkins's old friend and colleague from New York. Wagner said, "This is not a farewell meeting. It is merely the end of one chapter in the story of our friend and co-worker, Frances Perkins. Miss Perkins, our wish for you is this: May each succeeding chapter in your endeavors be as useful to the people of America as those that have gone before."

Perkins, now 65 years old, did not know just how the plot of the next chapter would unfold. But less than 10 days before the Mayflower dinner, it was clear her eyes were looking ahead to the final chapter. In a letter dated June 18, 1945, she sent directions for her funeral to an Episcopal clergyman. In the wake of the events of the past few months, she had obviously decided to take to heart some advice Roosevelt had given her years earlier: "Everybody ought to plan where he's to be buried. Otherwise they'll do the darnedest things to you."

A CAPACITY FOR LIVING AND GROWING TO ONE'S DYING DAY

In her biography of Franklin D. Roosevelt, Perkins expressed her admiration for his "capacity for living and growing that remained to his dying day." Perkins herself demonstrated this same capacity. In her final two decades she continued to live a rich professional and personal life.

In July 1945 she took a long vacation at the Perkins family home in Newcastle, Maine. There she was joined by her daughter Susanna, now a 29-year-old divorcée. Lovely as it was to relax as she hadn't been able to in years, she had pressing reasons to go back to work. From her Cabinet salary of $15,000 per year she had had to pay the expenses of her husband's care. And although that cost rose to $6,000 per year, she nonetheless always gave away a full tenth of her salary to charity.

On the day of Roosevelt's death, Perkins had been conferring with a State Department colleague on plans for U.S. representation at the next conference of the International Labor Organization (ILO). Perkins had been interested in this agency, which promotes the welfare of workers around the world, since its establishment in 1919. In 1934 she had urged Roosevelt to submit legislation,

RISKY
TIES

1902 STARTED
1. The Fund for the
Swimming Pool
2. Junior Lunches
3. Field

Although angered by Mount Holyoke's choice of a male president in 1937, Perkins participated in her 50th college reunion in 1952.

which Congress passed, authorizing the President to apply for membership in the ILO. At the ILO's annual conferences, delegates of each member country meet now as they did then to establish international labor standards on such matters as child labor and worker safety. When Harry Truman assumed the Presidency he asked Perkins if she would represent the United States at the October 1945 conference in Paris. She agreed.

Before she set sail, with Susanna as her traveling companion, she had been approached by the Viking Press, a New York publishing company, which offered her a contract to write a personal biography of Roosevelt. She rejected this offer. She had had a bad experience with an earlier publishing venture, *People at Work,* which, since its publication in 1934, she had always considered a "terrible book." She explained that a woman she knew (the sister-in-law of Paul Wilson's friend Henry Bruère), in search of work, had implored Perkins to let her go through her speeches and weave them together into a book. Perkins was upset by the outcome. "I mean, when the end came, it didn't quite bust our friendship, but that was because I made a determined effort not to allow it to." She dismissed the product as "a patchwork job" with "such cheesy, cheap, cheap—connective tissue that I couldn't stand it." Perkins rewrote a great deal of the manuscript, but she was unable to salvage the project. "It didn't make a good book out of it, but at least it spared me the humiliation of a thing that was so badly written that I couldn't endure." Although the reviewer for the *Springfield [Massachusetts] Republican,* at least, gave it a decent review, saying "Miss Perkins writes with spirit and has the knack of illustrating her arguments with concrete pictures and human incidents," the book was not a popular success. She was not eager to enter into another such exercise in futility.

But the publisher—eager to have the first Roosevelt biography on the market—was persistent. An agent of the publisher tracked her down at her hotel in London, where she stopped en route to Paris. Susanna convinced her mother to "stop being such a baby" and, somewhat reluctantly, Perkins signed the contract. She then promptly put the project out of her mind, but when she returned to the United States just before Christmas, the May 1st deadline for submitting the manuscript suddenly seemed almost upon her.

She spent most of the publisher's advance of $20,000 on a recording machine, a research assistant, and a few typists, but found herself unable to organize the masses of material that she was dictating and having typed. Thanks to the intervention of a friend who was also a literary agent she was saved from another literary disappointment. He recommended she hire as an editor the music critic for *The New York Times,* Howard Taubman. Recently released from the army and in search of a short-term, well-paying job, Taubman proceeded to make an outline and rewrite the material, transforming her memories into an appealing book.

The manuscript did come in a little late to the publisher, but all was forgiven when the book not only was well received by the press but also proved a fast-moving item in bookstores. Perkins took pleasure in recalling that the book reached the number-one spot on the bestseller list of the *New York Times,* where it remained for at least 10 weeks. As a result of the popular success of the book, Perkins received welcome royalty checks from the publisher, bringing in an additional several thousand dollars a year. Eleanor Roosevelt, in *This I Remember,* which came out three years later, gave Perkins's book a mixed review: "Frances Perkins, in her book, has drawn a wonderful picture of him that in many respects no one else could possibly have drawn. Yet even in her book, I think, there are little inaccuracies and misinterpretations, arising from the fact that each of us brings to any contact with another person our own personality and our own interests and prejudices and beliefs." But

PERKINS THE BIOGRAPHER

The Roosevelt I Knew *was well received by the public and critics alike. In this review, first published in* The Atlantic Monthly *in January 1947, the historian Arthur M. Schlesinger argued that Frances Perkins has discovered the key to writing a good biography: insight, humility, and verve.*

...Frances Perkins in *The Roosevelt I Knew* provides by far the best portrait of Roosevelt up to now. The very title of the book makes an instructive contrast with Elliott Roosevelt's [FDR's son's] easy assurance: *As He Saw It* [the title of Elliott Roosevelt's recently published book about his late father]—*The Roosevelt I Knew.* The humility is not only becoming but indispensable. There were many Roosevelts. Different people and different situations elicited different versions of that protean personality. But Frances Perkins's account of the Roosevelt she knew has so much maturity, discernment, and wisdom that it affords essential clues for anyone's Roosevelt.

Miss Perkins has no delusions about the completeness of her understanding. "Franklin Roosevelt was not a simple man.... He was the most complicated human being I ever knew...."

The lively and informative chapters on the early days of the New Deal make somewhat wry reading. The fertility of ideas and resource with which America attacked the depression stands in such melancholy contrast to the weariness and sterility which pervade Washington today in face of more urgent problems. Miss Perkins has, of course, an inescapable vested interest in many of the transactions she describes; and others who took part in the development of NRA... or the wages-and-hours legislation will occasionally quarrel with her emphasis. But she is neither pleading a case nor paying off grudges. . . .

The book has less to say about labor than one might expect, but it does suggest the enormous strides that have taken place since 1933... the cumulative effect of the book is to draw a picture of Roosevelt's mind in operation, a picture unsurpassed elsewhere in detail or perception. It confirms the absence of intellectual rigor and of elegance of taste which one has always suspected.... His reading was scattered and impressionistic. His taste even in painting, food, and movies was undiscriminating.

Yet these are all the standards of the intellectual, and Miss Perkins is too wise to regard them as decisive. Roosevelt simply "did not enjoy the intellectual process for its own sake."...

In short, Roosevelt remained peculiarly American in his intellectual operations—pragmatic, sentimental, experimental, indifferent to metaphysics, mistrustful of pure logic, impressed by anecdote and fact....

...Frances Perkins has discharged her obligation to historians with grace, fidelity, and insight. The temper and purpose of her book should serve as a model to the others who plan to write about the Roosevelts they knew.

Reprinted with permission of *The Atlantic Monthly*.

people continued to read *The Roosevelt I Knew* with pleasure, and it remains a "good read."

Her brush with literary success was not enough, however, to convince Perkins to become a professional writer. She was anxious to return to what she considered a real job: "I didn't want to succumb to this literary fantasy that goes around, you know, where you're a literary person and you go from one luncheon and one dinner and one tea to another." In fact, she never managed to bring to completion her only other attempt at a book. At the time of her death she was under contract to write *The Al Smith I Knew.* Although she tried to enlist Howard Taubman's assistance again, he was too busy this time. The mass of material she left behind became the basis of Matthew and Hannah Josephson's *Al Smith: Hero of the Cities. A Political Portrait Drawing Upon the Papers of Frances Perkins,* which was published in 1969.

Rather than flit from one literary event to another, she insisted, "I wanted to get to work.... I'd rather work at a thing, straightforward, a job." Luckily, although Truman had willingly seen her leave her Cabinet post, he recognized her for the fine administrator she was. Eager to put her experience to work elsewhere in his administration, on September 12, 1946, he appointed her to the Civil Service Commission. The Civil Service had been established in 1883 to make sure that government employment was open to all qualified citizens and that their career advancement was based on their merit, rather than limited only to those with political connections. Perkins remained a civil service commissioner until April 1953.

Her new job began auspiciously. The other two commissioners, both men, greeted their new colleague with a courtesy denied her by both her predecessor and her successor in the Department of Labor.

Perkins later described the duties of a civil service commissioner: to establish personnel guidelines; to compose entrance examinations; to provide the various departments with a list of persons who have already taken those exams, along with their grades; and to make sure that the appointing officers select appointees from among the top three names on the list.

These were not ordinary times to be a civil service commissioner, however. Although accusations that individual government employees were Communists out to subvert the Constitution were nothing new, as Perkins knew all too well, the onset of what is known as the cold war heightened the fear of Communists in government. The cold war is the term used to describe the bitter rivalry between the Soviet Union with its Communist allies (often called the Eastern bloc) and the United States with its democratic allies (often referred to as the Western bloc). The cold war began in 1945, following the end of World War II, and ended in 1992, when Russian President Boris Yeltsin and U.S. President George Bush formally declared that their countries did not consider each other enemies. As the cold war intensified in the late 1940s, many people in the United States came to believe that the search for Communist influences inside and outside the government was a contribution to the struggle against world Communism.

In addition to accusations of Communist connections being hurled at named individuals, the claim was now heard that the government of the United States was riddled with dozens, hundreds, or even thousands of unnamed Communists. Bowing to public pressure, on March 22, 1946, President Truman issued Executive Order 9835, which established a Federal Employees Loyalty and Security Program. All federal employees, whatever their jobs, were now to be subject to loyalty investigations, and anyone found disloyal would be denied a government position. It was a monumental task. The program officially began on October 1, 1947, and was ended when President

Eisenhower revoked Executive Order 9835 on April 27, 1953. In the more than five years between those dates the loyalty of 4,756,705 individuals was examined. This effort resulted in the removal from office or denial of employment on loyalty grounds to 560 individuals.

Although the program proved that charges that the federal government was a hotbed of subversive activity were untrue, it had a destructive effect on the morale of government employees. As Truman later noted in his *Memoirs,* "Many good people quit government rather than work in an atmosphere of harassment. And these reckless attacks have made it doubly difficult to attract good people to government service."

Many Americans viewed the loyalty program as a witch hunt in which slight, doubtful, or irrelevant evidence was used as an excuse to trample on the civil rights of innocent U.S. citizens. Perkins, however, looking back at that time, disagreed explicitly. "I would not use the word witch hunt," she said. "The truth was that during the war a great many people were taken in without any adequate investigation of their vouchers...the Government put them to work because there was such a vast need for people."

During the war Perkins herself had had the experience of discovering a young woman with Communist ties in the Department of Labor. The young woman had a sensitive position with the Bureau of Labor Statistics, working with figures that might have proven of military value if they had fallen into enemy hands. Although the young woman was very efficient at her job, Perkins charged her with incompetence. "It was incompetence in that she showed poor judgment in her outside contacts and in her affiliation with political groups that had a basic underlying philosophy contrary to that of the government of the United States. She was therefore incompetent to do the work for which she had been employed."

Perkins insisted that "a man has a constitutional right to

be a Communist, but he has no constitutional right to work for the Government of the United States." In this case, in fact, Perkins never claimed that the young woman should be dismissed from the Department of Labor because of her membership in the Communist party. "At that time it hadn't been established by the courts that membership in the Communist Party *ipso facto* made one a believer in the overthrow of the government by force and violence…. All I charged her with was bad judgment." After about "a week's excitement," a hearing was held, and the young woman was dismissed.

Following the issuance of Executive Order 9835, it became Perkins's responsibility to appoint a Loyalty Review Board, whose task would be to review cases on appeal. She had trouble finding not only a chairman but also members willing to sit on the board. "They withdrew, and they didn't want to do it, and they found excuses. They hated to do it. But we got a very fine assemblage of people eventually," including one woman. "Then they anguished over the cases." Perkins had no illusions that the Loyalty Review Board would make the correct adjudication on every case, but she did think that the chances of their doing so were good.

Among the Frances Perkins papers in Columbia University's Rare Book and Manuscript Library is a folder marked "United States Civil Service Commission Loyalty Review Board Cases." The folder includes Perkins's reasoning and recommendations on a variety of cases. In one case she argued that it makes no sense to bar an individual from government employment forever based on his having failed to report on official forms that he had briefly belonged to the Communist party as a young man. She contended that no one would think of barring him from government employment if he had failed to list on the form a brief membership in a drinking club of which he later became ashamed.

In a second case Perkins argued that it is improper to gauge a person's loyalty based on his unwillingness to inform against others. She added that it is improper for the government to tempt people to advance themselves by imperiling others.

Her review of another case led Perkins to argue that the Civil Service Commission's duty is to hire appropriate employees who will not harm the government, not to punish moral flaws in its employees. She also put that advice to use in another case, where she argued that socially unconventional behavior should not be confused with disloyal behavior. In that case she stated that a woman who cared for her fiancé in her apartment before they were married because she could not afford other medical care was not ineligible for government employment on those grounds alone.

However honorably she played her part in the Federal Employees Loyalty and Security Program, Perkins claimed that the bulk of her work in the Civil Service Commission dealt with much more routine matters. She took pride in the work she accomplished, including the development of a training program for "junior administrative assistants." Young people selected by their college professors as good candidates for government service were invited to take exams for entry-level administrative or scientific positions. Those who succeeded on the basis of the exams then underwent a six-month orientation period in which they were trained through a series of conferences and lectures. A number of people who went through the program turned out to be very capable government agency heads.

Although Perkins felt that being a civil service commissioner was not nearly as stimulating as being secretary of labor, it was nice for a change to be in a position where "you could go to bed at night and sleep comfortably without worrying about a strike that might break out in the borax mines or some such place as that." Summarizing her tenure at the Civil Service Commission, she said, "It proved to be much more interesting than I had anticipated."

In 1951, while Perkins was still with the Civil Service

Commission, her husband, Paul Wilson, now 76 years old, came to live with her in Washington. He was not the stimulating intellectual and social equal he had been when they had first met some 40 years earlier in New York. He had few interests now and had become very dependent on her. The following year, 16 days after his 77th birthday, Wilson died, "unexpectedly, after a long illness," according to the obituary notices. Perkins held the funeral at the Episcopal church in Newcastle, Maine, and had Wilson interred in the family burying ground there. In 1953, in order to fill out a widow's claim on Wilson's Equitable Life Assurance Society policy, she had to do a little research into his employment history. Reviewing old financial records confirmed her recollection that his last day of paid employment had been in early 1929.

At about the time Wilson came to live with her in Washington she was invited to participate in a project run by the Oral History Research Office of Columbia University. Over the period from 1951 to 1955 she was interviewed periodically in Washington. The result is a nine-volume history covering her life through 1953. The transcripts of the interviews, which make up *The Reminiscences of Frances Perkins,* fill more than 5,000 pages of double-spaced typescript.

Eight weeks before Wilson's death, the Democrats, who had occupied the White House for 20 years, were defeated in the Presidential election of November 5, 1952. Although President Truman had confounded the pundits by winning the election of 1948, this time a record turnout of voters gave a landslide victory to Dwight D. Eisenhower, who overwhelmed his Democratic opponent, Adlai E. Stevenson.

Just under a month later, on December 4, President Truman gave a farewell dinner to which Perkins, along with everyone else who had served in Truman's Cabinet or in the Cabinet he had inherited from Roosevelt, was invited. She found it a very disappointing event, which failed to mark in any significant way the conclusion of two decades of government achievement by Roosevelt and his successor. The gold plate on the tables failed to compensate for what she saw as a lost opportunity to turn the occasion into something truly memorable. As it was, it was merely a pleasant reunion. She lamented the fact that "the occasion just dribbled away without recognizing itself as an era which had finished."

On January 23, 1953, just after Eisenhower's inauguration, Perkins wrote a letter of resignation to him. She had the letter hand-delivered to the White House but heard nothing in response. Although she was uncertain about what she would do next, she was determined to "move out with dignity." When an offer came from the University of Illinois to give a series of 12 seminars on the labor department and the labor movement during the New Deal, plus a university lecture on *The Roosevelt I Knew,* she accepted. She thought it would be better to leave Washington than linger about, "having everybody in the Department telephoning to you what's being done now." On the literal eve of her departure, with her suitcases packed, she finally received "a very polite letter from Mr. Eisenhower saying that he thanked me for my services and so forth and accepted my resignation." In this undramatic fashion nearly 20 years of service to the federal government ended.

Perkins, whose career had begun in the classroom, spent the last 12 years of her life in academia. Presumably she had had a change of mind since reporting to her Mount Holyoke classmates in 1909 that she had "'thrown a hate' on teaching as a profession." In the spring of 1955 she left Washington for New York City, where she could be nearer her daughter, who had remarried in 1953, and her baby grandson. She then embarked on a series of lectures at the Salzburg, Austria, Seminar in American Studies; at the University of Bologna in Italy; and then closer to home at Cornell University in Ithaca, New York.

Perkins's lectures at Cornell were so well received that she was invited to be a faculty member at the university's School of Industrial and Labor Relations (ILR). There over the next nine years her colleagues and students referred to her as "Madame Perkins," little knowing how much that designation irked her. She rued the fact that the title "Madam Secretary"—a proper way to address a woman Cabinet member—had somehow been transformed into a title for her in ordinary life. "People who ought to know better use that combination of 'Madam' and 'Perkins.'... Being called 'Madam Perkins' is one of the things that gets me down. I don't know why."

Still, it is not hard to understand why the form of address seemed appropriate and stuck to her. As Professor Milton R. Konvitz, her younger colleague at the ILR school, recalled more than 30 years after Perkins's death, "Apart from the important public life that she had, she was inestimably outstanding as a person and personality. She was someone very special. If she came into a room where she was unknown, people would at once know that someone special had entered. She was recognizably an important person—her demeanor, her carriage, her style of dress, her eyes, everything about her marked her as someone very special. One was tempted to address her as 'Your Ladyship.' It seemed rude to talk with her as one would with any other woman, howsoever well bred, cultured, or highborn." And his wife, Mary, added, "Even socially F. P. was always introduced as Madame Perkins—because she was. Her

In 1956 Perkins joined the faculty of Cornell University's School of Industrial and Labor Relations. After her death the school established a named professorship in her honor.

143

voice was well bred and her manner impeccable—[she sent] a thoughtful thank you note for any hospitality."

In the spring of 1960 Perkins was invited by Cornell's 27 Telluride scholars, all male, to be the first woman guest in residence at the Telluride House on the university's campus. This group, among the university's most gifted, included both undergraduates and graduate students who held fellowships for intellectual ability from the Telluride Association.

An article in the *Telluride Newsletter* of January 1961 indicates how successful the match was between the 80-year-old Perkins and this group of young men, "whose manners" (according to the article's author) "have not always been described as impeccable." The author, Peter Mogielnicki, reported a number of benefits to the residents, ranging from the intellectual—"her frequent and welcomed discussions of current affairs"—to the aesthetic. Coming in to dinner one evening, the young men found a bouquet of flowers on one of the tables. Curious to learn who the donor of the blooms was, they examined the arrangement and discovered a gift card from the First Lady of the United States, Jacqueline Kennedy. It turned out that the flowers had been sent to thank Perkins for participating the previous weekend in a rally to plan the forthcoming Democratic campaign. Mentioning also her gift of fruit on another occasion, Mogielnicki alluded to an oft-repeated comment of Perkins's that being a woman had impeded her in life only in her attempt to climb trees. "In instances similar to these, Mme. Perkins has made it quite clear that although her being a woman has hindered her along the lines of decreasing her 'tree-climbing ability,' it certainly has been responsible for a delightfully motherly attitude on her part towards her 27 hosts." In 1963 the Telluride Association voted to grant Perkins permanent residence at Telluride House.

More than 30 years after spending time at Telluride

House with Perkins, one of her hosts, Abram Shulsky, recalled her as "a most remarkable woman" with "a tremendous reserve, but absolutely no stuffiness." He remembered her inviting a number of former colleagues for weekend seminars on the New Deal. Shulsky was particularly struck by the contrast between Perkins and James Farley—the Postmaster General (1933–40) and chairman of the Democratic National Committee (1932–40) who had thought she should deport Harry Bridges for the good of the party, whether the circumstances warranted it or not. While Perkins kept trying to analyze the various policies they had fought to enact, Farley had little to contribute on that subject. He could, however, remember how every member of Congress had voted on each critical issue. Although he was only a very young man at the time, Shulsky understood that Farley thought Perkins overly intellectual, and even perhaps a little tiresome. The undergraduate was thus even more admiring of her gracious and patient manner in dealing with her former colleague.

On March 4, 1963, exactly 30 years to the day after she became the first woman Cabinet member, Perkins participated in commemorating another important occasion: the 50th anniversary of the U.S. Department of Labor. In an animated conversation with President John F. Kennedy she demonstrated the size of the cockroaches she had found in her predecessor's desk on her first day as secretary of labor.

A little more than eight months later, on Friday, November 22, 1963, Perkins mourned with the rest of the nation upon learning of the assassination of the young President. Perkins had been invited to a dessert party that evening at the home of Professor and Mrs. Milton Konvitz. The event was canceled and Perkins left town, presumably to attend the funeral, on the night train, the *Phoebe Snow*. Before leaving she advised the Telluride Fellows that they should go ahead with their plans for the annual

At a 1963 dinner celebrating the 50th anniversary of the Department of Labor, Perkins shows President Kennedy the size of the cockroaches she confronted in her desk on her first day of work there.

Thanksgiving dinner, scheduled for that Sunday, to which, according to custom, they had invited faculty members and their families. Abram Shulsky recalled their uncertainty whether the event should proceed as scheduled. "In her typical stiff-upper-lip fashion, she ruled that it should."

The following year Perkins's health began noticeably to decline. She had been diagnosed a number of years earlier with hardening of the arteries and high blood pressure, and her vision was progressively worsening. By the winter of 1964–65 she was nearly blind. Her lecture notes had to be written in inch-high letters, and she could navigate familiar cities only by counting streets between obvious landmarks.

That spring she made a last trip to the Washington area, where she not only visited friends but also went on a retreat at the All Saints Convent in Catonsville, Maryland, south of

Baltimore. Since 1933 she had been taking periodic spiritual respite—praying throughout the day and otherwise observing the rule of silence—at the convent, a small community of Episcopal nuns. According to Alice H. Cook, a colleague at the ILR school, Perkins was at All Saints "when she had the stroke that led to her death."

Then she returned to New York City, where she stayed at the apartment of the same close friend who had selected the dress she had worn to Roosevelt's 1933 inauguration. With another old and intimate friend she went to a ballet performance featuring the stars Rudolf Nureyev and Margot Fonteyn, although her vision was too poor for her to appreciate the dancing itself. The following day she was admitted to Midtown Hospital in New York, where, over the next days, she suffered several strokes and went into a coma. Frances Perkins died on May 14, 1965.

The funeral service, which she had planned well in advance, was at New York's Church of the Resurrection. Eight Cornell Telluride scholars served as pallbearers. Perkins was buried in the family plot in Newcastle, Maine, between the graves of her husband, Paul Wilson, and her parents.

On May 18, the Episcopal Church at Cornell University held a requiem mass and memorial service for Perkins in the interfaith chapel in Anabel Taylor Hall. In her memory the Telluride Association created a Frances Perkins Memorial Fellowship in the School of Industrial and Labor Relations. A named professorship in her honor was also established at the school.

On April 10, 1980, the centennial of Perkins's birth, the United States issued a 15-cent stamp bearing her portrait.

Among the many tributes in her honor, one in particular summarizes the lasting achievement of this woman who had participated in so many of the formative events of 20th-century American history. Willard Wirtz, secretary of labor at the time of Perkins's death, said, "Every man and woman who works at a living wage, under safe conditions, for reasonable hours, or who is protected by unemployment insurance or Social Security, is her debtor."

CHRONOLOGY

April 10, 1880
Fannie Coralie Perkins is born in Boston, Massachusetts.

June 1902
Graduates with a degree in chemistry from Mount Holyoke College.

1904–1907
Volunteers with Chicago Commons and Hull House while teaching at the Ferry Hall School in Lake Forest, Illinois.

June 11, 1905
Enrolls in the Episcopal church in Lake Forest, Illinois, as Frances C. Perkins.

1907–1909
Serves as executive secretary of the Philadelphia Research and Protective Association.

1910
Receives a master's degree in political science from Columbia University.

1910–12
Serves as executive secretary of the New York Consumers' League, an affiliate of the National Consumers' League.

1911
Works with the New York State Factory Investigating Commission.

1912–17
Serves as executive secretary of the Committee on Safety of the City of New York.

September 26, 1913
Marries Paul C. Wilson in New York City, but retains her family name.

December 30, 1916
Gives birth to a daughter, Susanna, and becomes a working mother.

1917

Serves as executive director of the New York Council of Women for War Work.

1919–21

Appointed to the Industrial Commission of the New York State Department of Labor.

1921–22

Serves as executive secretary of the Council on Immigrant Education.

1923

Appointed to the Industrial Board of the state labor department.

1926–28

Serves as chairman of the Industrial Board.

1929

Appointed Industrial Commissioner of the New York State Department of Labor.

March 4, 1933–June 30, 1945

Serves as secretary of labor under President Franklin D. Roosevelt and for a brief period under President Harry S. Truman.

1934

Publishes her first book, *People at Work.*

January 24, 1939

A resolution is introduced in the U.S. House of Representatives demanding the impeachment of Perkins on a charge of conspiracy to avoid enforcement of deportation laws against Harry Bridges.

1939

Faces impeachment for failing to enforce deportation laws. Two months later the House of Representatives tables the resolution.

October 1945

President Truman sends Perkins to Paris as a government representative to an International Labor Organization conference.

May 1946

Publishes her second book, *The Roosevelt I Knew.*

1946–53

Serves as a U.S. Civil Service Commissioner.

1953

Begins a 12-year academic career by lecturing at the University of Illinois.

1956–65

Holds faculty position at the Cornell University School of Industrial and Labor Relations.

May 14, 1965

Dies in New York City.

April 10, 1980

On the centennial of Perkins' birth, President Jimmy Carter and Secretary of Labor Ray Marshall dedicate the headquarters building of the U.S. Department of Labor in Washington, D.C., to her memory. A 15-cent stamp is issued in her honor.

1980

Mount Holyoke College establishes the Frances Perkins Program to help women of a nontraditional age complete the requirements for a bachelor of arts degree.

1982

Inducted into the National Women's Hall of Fame in Seneca Falls, New York.

1988

Inducted into the Labor Hall of Fame.

1997

Governor William Weld of Massachusetts declares March 1, 1997, to be Frances Perkins Women in Politics Day.

FURTHER READING

BOOKS ABOUT FRANCES PERKINS

Colman, Penny. *A Woman Unafraid: The Achievements of Frances Perkins.* New York: Atheneum, 1993.

Lawson, Don. *Frances Perkins: First Lady of the Cabinet.* New York: Abelard-Schuman, 1966.

Martin, George. *Madam Secretary: Frances Perkins.* Boston: Houghton Mifflin, 1976.

Mohr, Lillian Holmen. *Frances Perkins: "That Woman in FDR's Cabinet!"* Croton-on-Hudson, N.Y.: North River Press, 1979.

Myers, Elisabeth P. *Madam Secretary: Frances Perkins.* New York: Julian Messner, 1972.

Severn, Bill. *Frances Perkins: A Member of the Cabinet.* New York: Hawthorne Books, 1976.

SELECTED ARTICLES ABOUT FRANCES PERKINS

Lord, Russell. "Madame Secretary: A Profile." *The New Yorker,* September 2, 9, 1933: 16-19, 20-23.

Macfadden, Bernard. "A Nationwide Demand for the Resignation of Madam Perkins." *Liberty,* Oct. 22, 1938: p. 4.

Stolberg, Benjamin. "Madame Secretary: A Secretary in Bewilderment." *Saturday Evening Post,* July 27, 1940: 9–11.

BOOKS AND SELECTED ARTICLES
BY FRANCES PERKINS

Perkins, Frances. *People at Work.* New York: John Day, 1934.

———. *The Reminiscences of Frances Perkins.* Unpublished memoir. Columbia University Oral History Research Office, 1951–55.

———. *The Roosevelt I Knew.* New York: Viking, 1946.

———. "My Job." *Survey,* March 15, 1929: 773–75.

———. "Some Facts Concerning Certain Undernourished Children." *Survey,* October 1, 1910: 68–72.

BOOK WITH SIGNIFICANT INFLUENCE
ON PERKINS'S CAREER

Addams, Jane. *Democracy and Social Ethics.* New York: Macmillan, 1913.

———. *The Spirit of Youth and the City Streets.* New York: Macmillan, 1910.

Riis, Jacob A. *How the Other Half Lives: Studies Among the Tenements of New York.* 1890. Reprint, New York: Dover, 1971.

BOOKS ABOUT PROFESSIONAL AND CULTURAL LIFE FOR U.S. WOMEN BEFORE WOMAN SUFFRAGE

Adickes, Sandra. *To Be Young Was Very Heaven: Women in New York Before the First World War.* New York: St. Martin's, 1997.

Filene, Catherine, ed. *Careers for Women.* Boston: Houghton Mifflin, 1920.

Deutsch, Sarah Jane. *From Ballots to Breadlines: American Women, 1920–1940.* New York: Oxford University Press, 1994.

BOOKS BY OR ABOUT HAROLD L. ICKES

Clarke, Jeanne Nienaber. *Roosevelt's Warrior: Harold L. Ickes and the New Deal.* Baltimore, Md.: Johns Hopkins University Press, 1996.

Ickes, Harold L. *The Secret Diary of Harold L. Ickes.* 3 vols. New York: Simon & Schuster, 1953–54.

Watkins, T.H. *Righteous Pilgrim: The Life and Times of Harold L. Ickes.* New York: Henry Holt, 1990.

White, Graham J. *Harold Ickes of the New Deal: His Private Life and Public Career.* Cambridge, Mass.: Harvard University Press, 1985.

BOOKS BY OR ABOUT FRANKLIN D. AND ELEANOR ROOSEVELT

Burns, James MacGregor. *Roosevelt: The Lion and the Fox.* New York: Harcourt Brace, 1956.

———. *Roosevelt: The Soldier of Freedom.* New York: Harcourt Brace Jovanovich, 1970.

Cook, Blanche Wiesen. *Eleanor Roosevelt, 1884-1933.* New York: Viking, 1992.

———. *Eleanor Roosevelt, 1933-1938.* New York: Viking, 1999.

Freedman, Russell. *Eleanor Roosevelt: A Life of Discovery.* New York: Clarion, 1993.

Goodwin, Doris Kearns. *No Ordinary Time: Franklin and Eleanor Roosevelt: The Home Front in World War II.* New York: Simon & Schuster, 1994.

Lash, Joseph P. *Dealers and Dreamers: A New Look at the New Deal.* New York: Doubleday, 1988.

———. *Love, Eleanor: Eleanor Roosevelt and Her Friends.* Garden City, N.Y.: Doubleday, 1982.

———. *Eleanor and Franklin: The Story of their Relationship based on Eleanor Roosevelts Private Papers.* Franklin Center, Pa.: Franklin Library, 1971.

Roosevelt, Eleanor. *This I Remember.* New York: Harper, 1949.

Roosevelt, Elliott, ed. *F.D.R.: His Personal Letters.* 4 vols. New York: Duell, Sloan, and Pearce, 1950.

BOOKS BY OR ABOUT ALFRED E. SMITH

Eldot, Paula. *Governor Alfred E. Smith: The Politician as Reformer.* New York: Garland, 1983.

Handlin, Oscar. *Al Smith and His America.* Boston: Little, Brown, 1958.

Josephson, Matthew, and Hannah Josephson. *Al Smith: Hero of the Cities. A Political Portrait Drawing upon the Papers of Frances Perkins.* Boston: Houghton Mifflin, 1969.

O'Connor, Richard. *The First Hurrah: A Biography of Alfred E. Smith.* New York: Putnam, 1970.

Smith, Alfred E. *Up to Now: An Autobiography.* New York: Viking, 1929.

BOOKS BY OR ABOUT OTHER ASSOCIATES OF FRANCES PERKINS

Cook, Alice H. *A Lifetime of Labor: The Autobiography of Alice H. Cook.* New York: Feminist Press, 1998.

Goldmark, Josephine. *Impatient Crusader: Florence Kelley's Life Story.* Urbana: University of Illinois Press, 1953.

Johnson, Hugh S. *The Blue Eagle from Egg to Earth.* New York: Doubleday, 1935.

Larrowe, Charles P. *Harry Bridges: The Rise and Fall of Radical Labor in the United States.* New York: Lawrence Hill, 1972.

McCullough, David. *Truman.* New York: Simon & Schuster, 1992.

Miller, Merle. *Plain Speaking: An Oral Biography of Harry S. Truman.* New York: Berkeley, 1973.

Morgenthau, Henry III. *Mostly Morgenthaus: A Family History.* New York: Ticknor & Fields, 1991.

Schorer, Mark. *Sinclair Lewis.* Minneapolis: University of Minnesota Press, 1963.

Ware, Susan. *Partner and I: Molly Dewson, Feminism, and New Deal Politics.* New Haven: Yale University Press, 1987.

BOOKS ABOUT THE U.S. DEPARTMENT OF LABOR AND THE CIVIL SERVICE

Altmeyer, Arthur J. *U.S. Department of Labor: The First Seventy-five Years.* Washington, D.C.: U.S. Government Printing Office, 1988.

Van Riper, Paul P. *History of the United States Civil Service.* Westport, Conn.: Greenwood, 1976.

INDEX

ACKNOWLEDGMENTS

I wish to thank a number of people for assisting me in the research and writing of this book. At a dinner in the home of my friend Professor Susan Dunn, the distinguished political scientist James MacGregor Burns first suggested to me that Perkins was a subject worthy of a new biography. I am grateful to both of them for launching me on a project that has proven so stimulating and pleasurable.

The texture of this book would have been much thinner were it not for the helpfulness and courtesy of the staff at Columbia University's Oral History Research Office and its Rare Book and Manuscript Library. I learned an enormous amount during the weeks I spent at Columbia's Butler Library in July and August 1997, reading through the thousands of pages of *The Reminiscences of Frances Perkins* and sorting through her many papers. I am very grateful to Columbia for permission to quote from Frances Perkins's oral history.

I am also indebted to Peter Carini, director of the Mount Holyoke College Archives and Special Collections, for guiding me through the Perkins materials in that collection. I thank Mount Holyoke for granting me permission to quote from the Frances Perkins Papers, Class Letter of 1902, Archives and Special Collections, Mount Holyoke College, South Hadley, Massachusetts, and from *The Mount Holyoke Alumnae Quarterly*. Also at Mount Holyoke, Professor Peter Berek put me in contact with Kay Althoff, director of the Frances Perkins Program at the college, who was kind enough to send me materials describing the program.

On a rainy Friday in May 1997, Radcliffe College archivist Jane Knowles eased me into my first collection of Perkins papers by helping me find my way through the materials at Radcliffe College's Schlesinger Library.

At the Registry Division of Boston's City Hall, Assistant Registrar Marie D. Reppucci gave me advice on how to procure a copy of the original birth certificate of Fannie Coralie Perkins, dated April 10, 1880.

The executive director of the Friends of the Department of Labor, Richard Conn, sent me material about the Labor Hall of Fame and about Frances Perkins's induction into it in 1988.

For helping me get a clearer picture of Perkins during her years at Cornell University, I would like to thank Abram Shulsky, who generously shared his memories of what it was like to be a Telluride scholar during the years that Perkins was a guest in Telluride House. My aunt and uncle, Professor and Mrs. Milton R. Konvitz, shed light on what it was like to know Perkins as a colleague at the School of Industrial and Labor Relations.

A number of individuals were kind enough to take the time to read through a draft of this book and to make valuable comments. I wish to thank Professor and Mrs. Milton R. Konvitz, Deborah Pasachoff, Eloise Pasachoff, Jay M. Pasachoff, Caitlin Rooney, Abram Shulsky, Joel Schwartz, Anna Schwartz, and Dorothy Segal.

At Oxford I wish to thank Nancy Toff, editorial director of Trade and Young Adult Reference, for her friendship and guidance; Casper Grathwohl, editor, for his assistance in the final stages of the book's preparation; and Joyce Berry, for securing the opening photo for Chapter 3.

Needless to say, whatever errors may remain in the book are my responsibility alone.

Finally, I am indebted to my family. My parents, Anna and Isaac Schwartz, welcomed me into their New York City home for the period during which I carried out my research at Columbia. I am eternally grateful not only for their hospitality on that specific occasion but also for their loving guidance over the decades. My husband, Jay M. Pasachoff, provided me with editorial advice and technical assistance during the book's many stages. My daughters, Eloise and Deborah, maintained a steady interest in Perkins over the months that the book was in progress. Each of these family members took time from his or her own professional commitments to assist me in my efforts. Deborah read other books about Perkins so that she would be well informed when the time came to edit my manuscript. Eloise served as my driver and traveling companion on my excursion to the Frances Perkins Archives and Special Collections at Mount Holyoke. Jay accompanied me to a variety of Frances Perkins sites in Worcester, Massachusetts, and obliged me by taking excellent photographs of a number of them. My gratitude to these family members for their love and support knows no bounds.

PICTURE CREDITS

Archive Photos: 65; The Bancroft Library, University of California at Berkeley: 96; Labor Management Documentation Center, Cornell University: 143; Susanna Coggeshal: 42-43; Corbis/Bettman: 56; Corbis/Bettman-UPI: 60-61; Library of Congress: 40, 59, 70, 80, 83, 91, 92, 104, 114, 119; Mount Holyoke College Archives and Special Collections: 8, 11, 13, 14, 38, 49, 130-131, 146; New York Herald Tribune: 101; Franklin Delano Roosevelt Library: 2, 94, 110, 112, 116; United States Department of Labor, Washington, D.C.: 22, 32, 68, 107; United States Postal Service: 147; Vanity Fair/Condé Nast Publications: 84

TEXT CREDITS

pp. 27–28: Perkins, Frances. "Some Facts Concerning Certain Undernourished Children." *Survey*, October 1, 1910: 68–72.

p. 51: Perkins, Frances. "The Factory Inspector." *Careers for Women*. Edited by Catherine Filene, 1920.

p. 76–77: Perkins, Frances. "The Cost of a Five-Dollar Dress." *Survey Graphic*, March, 1933.

p. 134–135: Schlesinger, Arthur M, Jr. "*The Roosevelt I Knew.*" (review) *The Atlantic Monthly,* January, 1947.

Naomi Pasachoff, a research associate at Williams College, has written over 20 books, including *Marie Curie and the Science of Radioactivity, Alexander Graham Bell: Making Connections,* and the collective biography *Links in the Chain: Shapers of the Jewish Tradition,* selected for the "1999 Books for the Teen Age" by the New York Public Library.